The Craigslist Killer

Crystal Majkowski

Published by Trellis Publishing, 2021.

THE CRAIGSLIST KILLER

First edition. July 13, 2021.

Copyright © 2021 Crystal Majkowski.

ISBN: 979-8224942497

Written by Crystal Majkowski.

THE CRAIGSLIST KILLER :

THE TRUE STORY OF MIRANDA BARBOUR

CRYSTAL MAJKOWSKI

The Story Behind "Craigslist Killer" Miranda Barbour

On December 3rd, 2013, Barbour was taken into custody by Sunbury, Pennsylvania police and charged with the murder of Troy LaFerrara, whom she had previously met through a Craigslist ad. Shortly afterward, she professed to have been a member of a satanic cult and murdering at least 22 people between the years 2008 and 2013.

Whether her claims of being a serial killer are to be believed or not, the details surrounding Miranda Barbour's life, arrest, and incarceration reveal a life of abuse and addiction. How did this young woman from Alaska, former classmate of Willow Palin, wind up a convicted murderer and self-professed serial killer in Pennsylvania?

Early Life

Miranda Barbour was born Miranda Kamille Dean on December 14th, 1994 in North Pole, a small town in the heart of Alaska that sits on the Tanana River. She lived there with her mother Elizabeth Dean, father Sonny Dean, and older sister Ashley Dean when she was a young child, until divorce and abuse tore apart her life.

Her personal nightmare began when her Aunt Melissa and Uncle Richard Fernandez moved just five houses down from their house in North Pole. Miranda was just a toddler at the time, and her Uncle Rick appeared to everyone like a loving brother and relative, a kind man who liked spending time with his two young nieces.

Miranda and her older sister Ashley began to spend every weekend at his house. Their Uncle Rick encouraged and arranged these sleepovers, and they went on for a year without question.

Around this time, Miranda began to complain often that she was in pain, but her parents did not recognize immediately the source of her discomfort—-her uncle's frequent sexual attacks. The sexual abuse went on for almost an entire year, until her older sister Ashley finally notified their mother of their uncle's "secrets." Their mother went to the police and Fernandez was arrested.

After a painful trial, Richard Fernandez was sentenced to 19 years for first degree sexual assault of a minor in 1998. But the justice system did not keep him incarcerated for long. He was released on parole after only serving nine years. The folly of this release was made apparent when he was found in possession of hundreds of images of child pornography in 2011, including a "how-to" manual that encouraged men to abuse their young family members and reflected on his own experiences with his nieces.

After this parole violation, he was sentenced to forty years in prison. But the damage had already been done.

The experience haunted Miranda for the rest of her life. In a Newsweek interview, Barbour stated about her uncle, "I think he created a monster inside of me. It's always there." She began to feel anger and violence bubbling up within her when she reached adolescence, coming out in the form of dreams, nightmares, and physical acts of violence. Although her mother Elizabeth helped her receive mental health treatment for her behavioral outbursts, Miranda still suffered.

Barbour described getting into a fight in middle school with former Alaska governor Sarah Palin's daughter Willow. The fight occurred because the governor's daughter would not move out of the way of Miranda's locker, she claimed, so she punched her in the face.

She was suspended briefly from school for this. She claimed she had reflected for a moment on her ability to murder Willow, but decided that her snobby behavior was not enough of a justification for the action.

In an interview with Dr. Phil McGraw, Miranda's sister Ashley stated that their mother Elizabeth had often invited many strange men over while they were young, ignoring her two daughters and leaving them alone at home when she left with these men. As the older sister,

Ashley was often left alone to watch Miranda, even when she was just a small child herself.

Barbour was still just an adolescent when she was became addicted to heroin. She was only twelve years old the first time that she ran away from home. Upon returning home, she told her mother that she had spent her time as a runaway, prostituting herself to survive. She also claimed that while she was away from home, she had met an older man named Forrest who was her "ruler." It was this obscure figure who supposedly introduced her to the satanic cult. According to her, Forrest was their leader.

Although Barbour claims the cult was a positive influence for her, helping her channel and control the rage she felt bubble up so often, she also claims that they were what led her to commit her first murder. According to Miranda's story, when she was just 13 years old, Forrest asked her to kill a man who owed him money. Supposedly, she solicited the man for sex in order to lure him down an alleyway. After they had arrived in the shadows away from the street, the cult leader helped her shoot him in the chest. She described how he helped her hold the gun and held his hands around hers to make her pull the trigger.

The murders supposedly continued after that. Not just in Alaska, either—-allegedly, Barbour committed murders with the cult in California, North Carolina, and Texas as well. She said most of her victims had been older men, however, she attested to one murder where the cult had tortured a woman in Alaska for prostituting her children. She also claimed that she had killed one man in self-defense while working at a club in Florida—-though it's unclear when she would have worked in Florida.

During this same time, Miranda claims she became pregnant. She tells a story of being drugged and tied to a bed, subject to an in-house abortion at the hands of the cult members, who did not want her to carry the baby to term. Eventually Miranda informed her mother of this incident. Upon hearing this, Elizabeth Dean had her daughter examined by a doctor, who informed her that there were "no signs of an ended pregnancy."

Miranda's parents confirm in interviews that their daughter spent these years moving in and out of treatment facilities for mental health issues, behavioral issues, and drug addiction. She made a handful of friends during her time spent in different facilities. She bounced back and forth between her father, mother, and an uncle on her mom's side, after her parent's divorce. Due to all of this, her teenager years were full of instability, and she was moved around from place to place.

In 2011, Miranda was pregnant again. She told *The Daily Item* that the baby belonged to Forrest, the cult leader. However, there is no father named on the birth certificate. She made the claim to newspapers and police that he had been murdered, however her parents later confirmed that Forrest was indeed still alive and inquiring about the parentage of Miranda's daughter.

The following year, a court placed Miranda in the custody of her Uncle Arlin Fletcher, and she moved to be with him and her mother in North Carolina. There, she gave birth to her daughter.

The situation was supposed to be a new beginning for her, on the other side of the country from where she had grown up. She began working as a cashier at a grocery store, and she signed up for a few college courses.

Upon arriving in North Carolina, she also met a boy, Elytte Barbour, and fell in love.

Elytte—-nicknamed Elf—-was a recent high school graduate from a North Carolina high school. Fellow classmates described him as weird and creepy, and a drug and alcohol abuser. He worked as a dishwasher at a local restaurant. When Miranda first arrived in the state, she met a fellow pregnant teen mother named Aimee Vaneyll, and they quickly became friends due to their similar situations. At the time, Elytte was Aimee's boyfriend, and he and Miranda met through Aimee.

Aimee would go on to describe her friend to *The Daily Item* as a satanist and "obsessed with sex." She

also said that Elytte shared Miranda's interest in satanism, however Miranda described that he was not able to be on the cult's "panel" because of Forrest's lingering presence in her life. Other individuals in her life, such as her mother, were unclear of what she meant by this.

The relationship between Aimee and Elytte didn't last. In March 2013, the two broke up. By June, Miranda and Elytte began seeing each other romantically. When Aimee was contacted by reporters during the investigation and trial, Miranda's old friend attested to no hard feelings between them about this.

Their relationship quickly became a whirlwind. In October, not even a month before the murder of LaFerrara and without much noted explanation, Miranda and Elytte eloped and quit their jobs. They had only been dating for about five months at this point. They grabbed all of their stuff and moved up to central Pennsylvania to live with friends. They chose rural Pennsylvania because of familial ties Elytte had there. While they lived there, Elytte eventually described to police that they earned income by posting jobs on Craigslist for Miranda to serve as a man's "companion" for money.

Despite the sound of the arrangements, Elytte insisted that this was not prostitution because Miranda was not having sex with the men. According to him, they simply met and had "delightful conversation."

This was what the couple was up to when they made their plan to utilize the same job posting service to intentionally lure someone to their death.

The Victim

The newlywed couple's murder victim was a middle-aged electrical engineer named Troy LaFerrara, who grew up in the rural town of Port Trevorton, Pennsylvania. He was born on June 20th, 1971 and attended Pennsylvania State University for civil engineering. He was licensed as a professional engineer, professional land surveyor, and sewage enforcement officer, and employed as an engineer at the Lycoming County Landfill by Cummings and Smith.

In 2003, LaFerrara met Colleen Keeney, and they dated for eight years before finally getting married in June of 2011. They did not have any children.

LaFerrara was an enthusiastic outdoorsman, heading out into the woods for hunting season, and practicing both archery and shooting rifles. He loved to practice target shooting and attended hunting shows on his days off.

Troy and Colleen had only been married for two and a half year/s when he was suddenly and tragically murdered, shocking the small rural Pennsylvania community.

The Craigslist Ad

Miranda and Elytte had been using Craigslist throughout October to arrange visits with men in order to make ends meet in Pennsylvania. The couple alleged that they actively spoke about killing together before, but did not immediately have any success with any of the men they scoped out for murder on Craigslist prior to LaFerrara.

The Craigslist ad that allowed the couple to land their mark was posted on November 1st, 2013. In the post, Miranda offered companionship to men who disliked their wives, exchanging payment for sex.

Troy LaFerrara was the unfortunate individual to answer her ad. She arranged to pay LaFerrara $100 for this encounter. In just a week's time, Miranda Barbour would follow through on her plan. The two would meet.

The Murder

The encounter happened on November 11th, 2013. Miranda met up with Troy LaFerrara in the parking lot of the Susquehanna Valley Mall in Hummels Wharf, Pennsylvania. He climbed into her vehicle, where Elytte was concealed on the floor of the backseat, covered in a blanket, carrying a cord, and waiting for the signal.

From the mall parking lot, they drove to the small city of Sunbury, Elytte hidden in the backseat the entire time. The couple had formulated a plan of attack prior to the encounter. They had decided on a code phrase that would serve as a sign for Elytte: "Did you see the stars tonight?" They had agreed that upon hearing those words, he would sneak up on LaFerrara from the backseat, wrap the cord around the man's neck, and strangle him to death.

But, as part of a twisted sense of justice, the couple had decided to give Troy one possible out by fabricating a story about her age. As the two sat in the front seat of the car, Miranda told Troy that she had lied to him about her age in the Craigslist ad. She falsely confessed to him that she had just turned 16 years old, framing herself as a minor.

This lie was meant to serve as a test for LaFerrara. And Miranda claimed that he did not pass. Allegedly, he informed her that the arrangement was fine, and that he still would have sex with her.

She then steeled herself to follow through with their original plan. He had not granted himself the out.

LaFerrara reached out to touch her thigh. Miranda asked the question that served as their signal, and Elytte rose in the backseat. He wound the cord around LaFerrara's neck and began to choke him, but he was hesitant. His lack of action drove her to pull out a knife and begin stabbing their victim. She drove the knife into Troy's chest twenty times, the cord still around his neck.

Once LaFerrara was still, the couple joined each other in the front seat. They turned on the vehicle and drove around for a while, seeking a location to dump the body they now had on their hands. They finally chose a residential backyard in the small city of Sunbury, and left LaFerrara's body there in the shadows, taking his wallet before they disappeared.

The rest of their night's actions were intentional and celebratory. The newlyweds visited a department store together and purchased cleaning supplies: bleach wipes, towels, and cleaning spray. They worked together to scrub the blood from the car's passenger seat, attempting to remove the evidence and get away with their crime, confident in their ability to do so.

The couple then made the hour drive to the state capitol, Harrisburg, where they ate dinner and spent time celebrating at a strip club, filled with an adrenaline rush and in high spirits. It was actually Elytte's 22nd birthday, and they were determined to do something nice for it, although Miranda would later claim in interview that the strip club they attended was lame.

On the morning of November 12th, Sunbury residents stumbled across the discarded body of Troy LaFerrara in the backyard. The police began their search for who killed him—-and why. Meanwhile, the Barbours continued their lives as if they had done nothing wrong. Elytte purchased Miranda a wedding ring from Zales, possibly using money that had nabbed from LaFerrara's wallet, and she flaunted it in a Facebook post just several days after the murder.

The police were able to quickly pick up on their trail when they located LaFerrara's cell phone. On the phone were texts between Miranda and Troy, revealing the details of the arrangement, as well as some details about who she was. The murderous couple had been sloppy, unprofessional, and careless—-despite Miranda's claims that she had done this up to 20 other times. The police had more than enough evidence to locate and arrest her.

They tracked down Miranda just three weeks later on December 3rd and arrested her. Her husband Elytte was arrested three days later.

The Motive

Despite the later landslide of information that Miranda Barbour would offer, initially upon arrest the couple denied ever meeting Troy

LaFerrara, or even knowing who he was. However, the last call made on the victim's phone was to Miranda. The evidence was clear, and the murder was difficult for the Barbours to deny for long.

At first, Miranda claimed that the murder had occurred in self-defense. She said that LaFerrara had tried to sexually assault her, and that they had simply killed him to protect her. The couple pleaded not guilty to first degree murder charges, which included the threat of the death penalty.

As the investigation continued to press the Barbours with questions, eventually the truth came out. Both Elytte and Miranda Barbour confessed to police that they had been plotting to kill someone together for months. The police affidavit reveals that the couple explained that LaFerrara's murder occurred because they wanted to bond over the experience of killing another human being together. They believed that the experience would make them closer than ever as a couple.

The newlyweds claimed that they had planned several other attempts to kill before, but none of them had been successful. Whether this was because of a situation such as Miranda offering an out, like she did with LaFerrara, is unclear. What is clear is that the couple timed the murder to fall on their three week wedding anniversary, and they were successful in following through with their plans. The fact that they had gone out and celebrated Elytte's birthday afterward was damning as well.

The murder was meant to be fun, a bonding experience.

On August 26th, 2014, during a status conference at the Northumberland County Court, the couple both pleaded guilty of second-degree murder.

In subsequent interviews, and to police, Miranda Barbour insisted that the murder would not have taken place if Troy LaFerrara had answered her correctly when she lied to him about being a minor. She said that if he had given the right response, she would have let him go.

Her reasoning for her crime was filled with a harsh bitterness toward the legal system that had failed her. In an interview with Newsweek, Miranda stated, "The legal system is supposed to protect people from these people. It doesn't. It didn't protect me." Her responses revealed how her uncle's horrific abuse and release from jail had affected her, and how she justified her actions based on this experience, using her uncle's abuse and release as an example of the system's dysfunction.

But the information didn't stop there. Miranda went from denying everything, to confessing that LaFerrara had not been her first kill. In fact, she revealed to police that he had been just one of many people that she had murdered for similar reasons. She told the police and newspapers that the number of victims could range anywhere between 22 to 45 people—-that she had stopped counting eventually.

Miranda's claim was met with disbelief by the police. However, Miranda insists she is telling the truth, even claiming that if law enforcement were to ask, she could draw maps to where the bodies hid.

Her professed reason for such a high body count appears to be tied to two things: her participation in the satanic cult, and her desire to punish people who took advantage of minors—-including the dark rage she claims consumed her after the abuse she faced at the hands of her uncle.

Is Miranda Barbour a Serial Killer?

If her claims are to be believed, Miranda Barbour is quite a prolific serial killer. Her story drew a lot of media attention, questions about this potential new serial murderer flooding in. The Northumberland County District Attorney Anthony Rosini made a statement that the county had contacted other law enforcement agencies in the places where she had lived, and these agencies had no information that backed up any of Miranda's claims. The Alaska State Troopers declared that there existed no evidence that she had ever murdered anyway during her time in that state.

Her family members were skeptical as well. Elizabeth Dean stated that she didn't believe her daughter had murdered anyone other than Troy LaFerrara, especially considering how sloppy that murder had been done—-a reference to leaving the cell phone behind and being caught so easily. Her sister Ashley expressed the same doubt.

Her father Sonny said that there was no way she had killed anywhere near 22 people, but he could entertain the possibility that she may have killed some person while living in his home in Alaska. The reason he thought this was a possibility was because she had run away from home for days at a time at least twice—-and he count not account for her whereabouts during that time.

Both of her parents described her as manipulative and a liar. Her father described how he believed she lived in a fantasy world—-how all of these things just happened inside her head, but not in reality. He called her selfish, and said that she craves attention, that being the motivator behind her actions.

Both her father and sister publicly stated that if the court were to find the death penalty appropriate for Miranda, that they would support this. They believed that she should face the consequences for her crime.

Old friends of Miranda corroborated that she had been involved with some sort of group, but that she had not called it a satanic cult, but a gang. She told her friend Alex, who she met while in treatment at a facility, that the gang was made up mostly of men.

Miranda insists that she has never been more honest than when confessing to her murders and crimes. She told reporters that while it hurt that these people did not believe her, she was able to laugh it off.

Incarcerated

The trial for the murder of Troy LaFerrara was held on September 18th, 2014 in a courthouse in Northumberland County, Pennsylvania. At the trial's conclusion, Miranda and Elytte Barbour both received a life sentence without parole for second-degree murder, aggravated assault, robbery, and possession of an instrument of crime. At the time of their sentencing, Miranda was only 19, and Elytte was 22 years old.

The judge declared that their permanent removal from society was necessary.

The two convicted murders sat in the courtroom as they were sentenced, stoic, faces devoid of emotion. During the trial, they listened to stories of grief from the victim's family members, without expression.

Miranda was sent to Lycoming County's state women's prison, to live alongside other women with life sentences. Elytte was sent to the State Correctional Institution at Forest.

While incarcerated, Miranda Barbour confessed that she thought about wanting to die. She said that she knew at some point she was going to be locked away. She described herself plagued with regret. The regret that she felt was for the pain she had caused her family, and for her own reputation, that she had damaged so thoroughly. But she also brought up her husband and daughter, who she had lost custody of after being arrested and charged with murder. She regretted the fact that she might not ever be able to hold them again, and wished that she had more time to say goodbye to them.

However, her regret does not extend to her victim, Troy LaFerrara. She still insists that he deserved to die, and that she never hurt anyone who didn't deserve it. In her perspective, the murder that she committed spared girls from sexual abuse, something that the justice system was not able to do. She continues to justify her actions as an act of saving grace for the potential victims of the men she killed.

In June, 2016, Miranda filed for divorce from Elytte Barbour, having not seen him since she was arrested back on December 3rd, 2013. She claimed that their inability to see each other, incarcerated in two different facilities, had "irretrievably broken" their marriage.

After her arrest, Miranda's daughter spent some time in Snyder County protective services in Pennsylvania. Various family members fought for custody of the toddler in the years following her arrest and conviction.

In prison, Miranda spends her time reading books and writing letters. She says that older men send her fan mail, asking her for small requests, like to simply say their name. But this is her life now, and she will spend the rest of her days incarcerated for her crime.

Internet Serial Killer

Thomas Griffin

Serial killers are a fascinating subject to the public. On one hand, we as a collective society are frightened by their horrific murders and indignant at how their heinous lives lasted for so long. On the other, we are fascinated by their complex lives and remarkable ingenuity—if anything, reading about them puts us temporarily in the mind of the killer themselves, simultaneously disgusted and a voyeur nonetheless. Maybe we just want to avoid situations for practical sakes where a trusting face may appear and help us recognize the signs of someone capable of these egregious crimes; other times, there's a voyeuristic *pleasure* that fuels our innate instincts.

This sentiment may not be more apropos for the serial killer **John Edward Robinson**. Known as the "Internet's first serial killer," he embodied a con man's savvy with reckless precision, taking at least eight women down his path until his conviction in 2003.

Early Life

It is the nature vs. nurture question: was this person born this way, or did their upbringing cause irrevocable harm and set them on the path of harming others. For John Edward Robinson, the analysis only offers more questions than it solves.

Born on December 27th, 1943, Robinson was reared into a middle-class suburban upbringing of Cicero, Illinois. The middle child of five children, with an alcoholic father employed in a blue-collar job as a machinist at Western Electric, and a strict, disciplinarian mother that pushed him towards success, his upbringing was relatively unremarkable. As a member of the Boy Scouts and later the Eagle Scouts, his troop even gave a variety show performance for England's Queen Elizabeth II. In 1957, he enrolled at Quigley Preparatory Seminary, a private school that trains young boys for priesthood, but he dropped out after a year for disciplinary issues.

By 1961, with priesthood not a fitting career, Robinson enrolled at Morton Junior College (also in Cicero) to train as a medical X-ray technician. He also married at the age of 21 to a woman named Nancy

Jo Lynch, so it seemed he was on his way towards attaining a normal life. He would drop out of Morton Junior College after two years, however, and move to Kansas City, MO.

It is at this point that we begin to see his "descent" into criminal behavior. Despite not having proper credentials, he managed to fake his way into a position at a prominent medical office. However, it wasn't just any medical office that he managed to become employed at; it was at Wallace Graham's office, the personal doctor of President Harry Truman. While those stakes may have been high to begin with, he had other plans in mind. All the while working surreptitiously, Robinson was embezzling funds for his own personal use by manipulating deposits and checks. Eventually, he was caught after embezzling nearly $33,000, sentenced to three years of probation and only found guilty of "stealing by means of deceit."

John Edward Robinson didn't stop there, however. Following his sentencing, he found employment at a television-rental store. Despite probation, he was found to be stealing merchandise and fired, but not brought up on criminal charges.

In 1970, he moved back to the Chicago area, unbeknownst to (or permitted by) his probation officer, gaining employment as an insurance salesman. By 1971, he was once again brought up on charges for embezzlement from the insurance agency that hired him and was subsequently ordered back to Missouri.

His sentencing was once again lenient, Robinson was given only an extended probation. In 1975, Robinson's probation was extended further yet after another arrest for securities and mail fraud related to a fake medical consultation business he formed in Kansas City.

Then, not declaring that he was on probation, he managed to find a systems analyst position at Mobil Oil Corporation. Remarkably, his probation officer even endorsed his new lifestyle by stating for the parole board that Robinson "does not appear to be an individual who is basically inclined towards criminal activities and is motivated towards achieving middle class values." In addition, another officer later stated that Robinson was "responding extremely well to probation supervision," and that she was "encouraging [Robinson] to advance as far as possible with Mobil Oil." Weeks after these glowing statements, Robinson was found to be stealing nearly 6,000 stamps from the company and was promptly fired.

"He did not work any type of legitimate job," Lt Rick Roth said. "Where he did not take steal the company for some kind of money."

If you're scratching your head at how this was permissible, remember that we're only covering some of the larger cons that he was involved with—in fact, his early track record is even more checkered the closer one looks into it—worse, we may never know the full extent of his prolific con man's life. While his story may seem to be a tamer version of "Catch Me If You Can"—Robinson was clearly an intelligent person—he demonstrates his ability to straddle the line between crime and appeasing society, cleverly blending his way in. For most people, these early convictions may have been crippling, but he clearly used deceit to achieve a place in society that would fuel his future crimes. Perhaps what is the most enraging is seeing how a clever person could evade authorities time and time again—weren't their mechanisms in place to prevent Robinson from committing the same crimes, time and time again? However, while he was "fooling" authorities, WORSE crimes were being committed using this same intelligence.

Beginning of the Murders

While he was committing the cons, John Edward Robinson was known ostensibly as a pillar of the community and a dedicated family man, now raising three children with his wife. Consistent with his days of youth, he became a Scoutmaster and a Sunday school teacher. Using his con man abilities to bolster himself in the community, he persuaded the board of directors of a local charitable organization by forging letter from the mayor of Kansas City (and other civic leaders) to their executive directors, commending his volunteering efforts and his status as a model citizen. He then orchestrated that he be placed as "Man of the Year" in 1979, throwing a festive awards luncheon in his own honor. Of course, this honor didn't go unchecked, especially as the Kansas Star reported on this event positively, and then retracted it when Robinson's track record of embezzlement came to light—tarnishing the reputation of a reporter and the newspaper's fact-checking mechanisms.

Of course, Robinson persevered, fooling those not familiar with anything more than the mask and image he was trying to present. With this facade in place, he used it as a front for his activities. He began to openly proposition the wives of his neighbors for sex, on one occasion causing a fist fight. Robinson also joined a secret sadomasochism cult called the International Council of Masters, becoming its "Slavemaster." The duties of the Slavemaster included luring victims to gatherings to be tortured and raped by cult members.

To serve these purposes and his own, he started more fraudulent shell companies named *Equi-Plus* and *Equi-2*. Nineteen-year old Paula Godfrey was the first victim of Robinson's plans, where he hired the unemployed and financially desperate woman to supposedly work as a sales representative. She, in turn, left for "training" under Robinson's wing, and then disappeared, her family uncertain of her whereabouts. Her family sent out a missing persons report. Robinson then typed up a letter in Godfrey's behalf, stating that she was doing fine and that she didn't want to see her family.

Godfrey remains "missing" to this day.

By 1985, Robinson met Lisa Stasi and her four-month-old daughter, Tiffany, at an abused women's shelter, offering her a promise of employment in Chicago. He offered her an apartment and daycare for her baby. It was an offer too good to refuse (or too good to be true). In turn, Robinson asked her to sign several sheets of blank stationery, as he convinced her that she would not have the time to do so as they would be traveling extensively. Simultaneously, Robinson contacted his brother and sister-in-law, unable to adopt a child through the traditional channels, and offered them a child whose mother had committed suicide. Charging them $5,500 in made-up fees, Robinson's brother and sister-in-law adopted Tiffany along with a set of forged adoption papers.

Lisa Stasi was never heard from again.

The Stasi family would receive a phone call from someone who a priest from the City Union Mission in downtown Kansas City. The priest called himself "Father Martin" and stated that he had seen Lisa and Tiffany, describing them as "doing fine" but they had left town with "a guy named Bill."

The family tried to verify the story, calling the mission back.

They are then told that there is no "Father Martin" at the mission.

Police would investigate, questioning Lisa's former husband who had a solid alibi. They also interviewed Robinson.

"He told me, yeah, she was referred to me," Detective Chuck Wilson recalled Robinson telling him. "I said I would put her up in my Kansas City outreach program. Lisa came to his office with a young man by the name of Bill who she said was her new boyfriend and that they were going to go off togethr and they were going to start a new life and she really thanked Robinson for all of his help and for being there to support her but she really thought things were coming together and she was really going to start a new life."

"Bill" and "Father Martin" were just names that Robinson used to throw the authorities off his trail.

Robinson's depravity didn't stop there. Twenty-seven year old Catherine Clampitt left her child with her parents in Wichita Falls, Texas in 1987. She moved to Kansas City to find employment and a better life for her family. Answering an ad placed by Robinson, she fell for the same trap as the previous women.

Clampitt would answer the ad that wanted an "executive secretary" who would work for a "busy CEO" named "John Dawson."

After answering the ad, Clampitt would vanish.

Clampitt's mother, however, would receive a typewritten letter purportedly from her daughter. The words do not sound like things her daughter would say. Her mother grew concerned and had Catherine's stepbrother call her workplace to speak with "John Dawson."

He is told that there is no "John Dawson" working there.

Clampitt's brother goes through her belongings and finds a hotel receipt signed by a John Robinson. Doing his own due diligence, he discovers that John Robinson owns the company that Clampitt went to work for, Equis II.

Clampitt's mother then goes to the company headquarters only to find out that the place has been closed down and that Robinson had been arrested earlier for fraud and theft.

"He was just a small-time con man," FBI agent Jeff Daniels said. "There was no indication that he had been involved in anything really much more than that."

Robinson benefited from the fact that all the detectives worked by hand and not via computers as they are now. Detectives were unable to make the connection between Godfrey, Stasi and Clampitt.

All three cases eventually go cold.

Clampitt's remains have not been found and her missing persons report remains open.

Incarceration and Next Phase

As most criminals (and especially serial killers) tend to, Robinson began to get careless. Between the years of 1987 to 1993, he was incarcerated in Kansas and Missouri for his multiple fraud convictions and parole variations. While this incarceration would be believed to reduce his criminal activities, it only increased his focus. At Western Missouri Correctional Facility, he managed to ingratiate himself to Beverly Bonner, the 49-year-old prison librarian. He must have been incredibly persuasive, as upon his release, Bonner left her husband and moved to Kansas to be employed by Robinson. This was all a set-up for Robinson's next plan, as he funneled Bonner's alimony checks to be forwarded to a Kansas P.O. Box. As a pattern from the previous women, her family never heard from her again. The checks kept arriving, being forwarded from Bonner's mother, and they were cashed—by Robinson, of course.

The Internet's Roleplay

Robinson was always on the lookout for the next scam to fuel is sadistic impulses. By his release in 1993, the Internet was readily available to the general public and a person of Robinson's intelligence was sure to take advantage of its wide reach. He roamed chat rooms and social networking sites, under the alias of his former sadomasochistic cult title, "Slavemaster," intent on finding women who were interested in submissive sexual roleplay amid the BDSM lifestyle (an acronym that blends "Bondage and Discipline" "Dominance and Submission" and "Sadism and Masochism" under one catchall).

The first victim he met online was forty-five year old Sheila Faith. Sheila had a 15-year-old daughter Debbie that was disabled, confined to a wheelchair due to spina bifida. Robinson managed to portray himself as wealthy and altruistic, offering to support both of them—offering Sheila a job and paying for Debbie's therapy. Sheila was convinced and moved from Fullerton, California to Kansas City.

Both mother and daughter immediately disappeared.

Faith's pension checks were dutifully cashed—by Robinson for the next seven years.

His crimes didn't stop there as the Internet only increased his reach. Robinson was beginning to develop a name for himself in the BDSM community, which not only was increasingly popular, but blurred the line between what actually qualified between consent and abuse.

By 1999, he found another victim, a 21-year-old Polish immigrant living in Indiana named Izabela Lewicka. She was an intellectual, often frequenting bookstores and being regarded as a regular patron by the staff of one bookseller in particular. Much like Sheila, he offered her employment and a bondage relationship, which she agreed to by filling out a 115-item "slave contract," giving Robinson carte blanche over nearly every aspect of her life, including her bank accounts and financial freedom.

To ensure her trust and to put up further smokescreens, Robinson bought her an engagement ring—he was still married—and brought Izabela to the county registrar, where they paid for a marriage license. For an immigrant, this cemented her citizenship, but the license was never picked up (nor was it valid). At her last appearance at the bookshop she frequented, Izabela was spotted with Robinson, purchasing a number of books and announcing that she was now married to him. Izabela also informed her parents that she was married, but it is unclear whether this was another orchestration by Robinson. By the summer of that same year, Izabela had disappeared. To cover his tracks, he told one of his hired web designers that she was caught smoking cannabis and was subsequently deported.

Dovetailing with Izabela's disappearance, Robinson convinced yet another victim into his BDSM desires. Suzette Trouten, a licensed practical nurse that moonlighted as a submissive slave. Again, using the Internet and the powers of his persuasion, he managed to convince Trouton to move from Michigan to Kansas so that the pair could travel and pursue their relationship.

"Suzette Trouten had told her family that she was going to work for a wealth businessman who did a lot of international traveling," Detective Wilson said. "And that she was going to take care of this businessman's ailing father while he traveled."

Like Clampitt's mother, Trouten's mother Caroline takes the bull by the horn and calls her "employer" when she has not heard from Suzette.

She is told that Suzette had run off with a man named "Jim" who was going to be sailing around the world with her.

"Suzette Troutten was a momma's girl," Lt. Rick Roth said. "Was always in contact with her mom either through e-mail or the telephone. Caroline knew that her daughter would call her and fill her in on what was going on. She knew something terrible had happened to her."

Again, Robinson mailed letters to cover his tracks, these letters purportedly to be from overseas, but postmarked with Kansas City postmarks. To further cover his behavior and Trouton's lack of correspondence, Robinson confided in her mother that she stole money from him and ran off with an acquaintance.

The Arrest of John Edward Robinson

"At the time he was supposedly running a business," Roth said. "That was basically a magazine for mobile home trailer parks."

The FBI and police were dumbfounded at how to build their case. They had missing women all connected to a two bit con man but had no physical evidence.

"We had to find all of these individuals," FBI Agent Dirk Tarpley said. "Make sure number one that they were alive and find out what find out what kind of contact he was having with them. What was he trying to do."

Suzette's mother would continue to receive letters. She knew that Suzette was not writing the letters as there were no spelling errors and the fact it "just didn't sound like Suzette."

Police were convinced, however, that Robinson was involved in her disappearance. They didn't want to start interrogating just yet. Instead, they began to question Suzette's friends.

"Suzette Trout was kind of a free spirit," Roth said. "She was into the BDSM lifestyle. She was always on the Internet with people in that lifestyle and she was ready to be on her own."

"None of us really knew anything about it (BDSM)," Roth continued. "So as we're conducting this case we're trying to learn about this lifestyle. Pain is part of this lifestyle. So slapping or spanking someone, that's natural."

Friends would reveal that Suzette liked to be the "sexual submissive".

She spend a lot of time surfing the Internet looking for a "master."

"She had come to this area at the behest of this guy named John Robinson," Lt Paul Morrison said.

John Robinson, however, did not look the part. He was a con man, yes. But a killer?

"Our impression of John Robinson was that he was a small-time con artist who was involved in a number of con schemes over the years," Daniels said. "But nothing really more than that."

But Robinson had a "side business", continually calling hospital and charity homes inquiring about helping out single mothers or other women in trouble.

Determined to not let Robinson off the hook, the FBI mounted an exhaustive investigation.

"We called in all the old retired detectives," Roth said. "Everyone who worked his cases before, trying to find a probation officer, we were looking into his (Robinson) background to find any clues that we could use against him.

The FBI began to focus on Tiffany Stasi, the baby. By the time they amped up the investigation in 2000, the baby would be fifteen years old.

And the FBI believed that somehow the baby would still be alive.

Initially, they believed that Robinson might be in some kind of baby-selling ring. An informant would come forward, however, and reveal that he would bird-dog women for Robinson. They discovered that Robinson would hire women for "photo sessions" and believed that he may have been selling this women into prostitution across international lines.

"It was hard to figure out what he was doing," Daniels said. "He was a con man on one hand but on the other hand he seemed to be involved in these other things which were darker."

The FBI was at a loss as they only had circumstantial evidence. They then put Robinson on twenty-four hour surveillance.

"We didn't want to tip our hand at any time to let Robinson know," Roth said. "If we contacted him, the gig was up and he would start denying everything and possibly sending us on goose chases."

They needed watch Robinson and wait for him to make a mistake.

They quickly learn he's living a double life. During the day, he is a family man with four kids. At night, he is with the underworld characters of topless bars and the like.

"We followed him to homes," Roth said. "We followed him to motels where he had women meet him there. The man was just in total action until five o'clock when his wife got off work."

"Robinson thought he was smarter and brighter than anyone else," Wright said. "That if he got caught he would just tell another lie as he had done for so many years and he didn't believe that there was anyone that was going to hold him accountable."

The FBI did a wire tap on his phone and subpoenaed records for his Internet usage. The FBI was able to log in to two Canadian women who were having real time correspondence with Robinson.

He was inviting the women over for BDSM sessions.

"To me he just seemed like a very commonplace little man who you would never suspect being involved in S&M type activities," Wright said.

"He referred to himself in the e-mails on the BDSM club website as 'master'," Roth said. "And that's what we knew him as. The 'Slave Master.'"

His modus operandi remained the same over the last fifteen years. He would seduce women with his BDSM techniques than promise them a job.

"He promised them the moon," Roth said. "And a lot of these women just took it, were hooked and came to Kansas City."

The FBI soon set up a stakeout at the motel where Robinson would indulge with the women he would import from out of town.

"They could hear talking," Wright said as the FBI agents listened outside his room. "A man's voice. A woman's voice. They heard what they thought were some slaps. We knew that he was into this BDSM lifestyle and that probably was taking place in that room. It was a really tense time for law enforcement because you knew somebody was getting hurt but the question was what was consensual and when did it cross the line."

Robinson's carelessness continued, perhaps as he felt more and more convinced of his abilities to evade authorities. Fortunately, he was not aware that he was building a case against himself while police carefully orchestrated a plot to track him down. His name was becoming linked to more than one missing person report. By 1999, both Kansas and Missouri began to implicate him as being involved.

His addiction to sex would prove to be his undoing as two women filed sexual battery complaints against him in June of 2000.

A woman named Brenda would come forward.

"She had come to town to work for a man she knew as James Turner," Roth recalled. "She was down on her luck, she was unemployed at the time, had no money."

When Brenda meets up with "James Turner", however, she realizes that she has gotten in over her head.

"One of the times they had gotten into an argument," Roth said. "She was struck by him. A little too hard. She had went up to the desk to inquire who had rented the room and she was told 'James Robinson.' So she knew that something wasn't right."

Brenda would go to police and accuse Robinson of sexual battery.

Another woman would come forward, filing an identical complaint against Robinson as well as robbery (he allegedly stole nearly $900 worth of sex toys.)

Buoyed by the two complaints, police now have enough to arrest Robinson.

Police arrested him at his rural property near La Cygne, Kansas.

"We were all a nervous wreck," Detective Wright recalled. "It was all very tense and a nervous time for everybody. He answered the door. We knocked on it. Was polite. You know, kind of carefree, invited us in. We told him that he was under arrest. We told him that we'd be investigating him for quite a while."

Robinson is arrested for sexual battery and robbery. But the investigators decide to question him about the missing women.

"Robinson turned pale," Wright recalled. "He started almost hyperventilating. I remember he turned back and looked at me (and said) 'Jesus Christ' like that and just kinda collapsed in the chair. I think it was a real shock to him and I think he knew would had him but when we walked him out of the house he picked himself back up and he was kind of back up and he was back to his arrogant self and he said 'you guys are making a big production out of this, aren't you?'"

The authorities confiscate his computers and get search warrants for the various storage units he has in four different cities.

"The Olatha storage locker proved to be a treasure trove of evidence," Lt Morrison said. "We found birth certificates, driver's licenses, social security cards belonging to several of these women. The kinds of things that you don't give up unless you're dead. It sort of confirmed what we were thinking all along and that is where are these letters coming from?"

They still had no bodies, however.

Searching his farm, a task force came upon two decaying bodies, hidden in eighty-five-pound hazardous-material drums.

"We actually were going to move the barrels out in order for the dog to get scent there," Roth said. "And when I rolled the barrel out and brought it upright, we saw blood coming out."

The bodies inside were identified as two of the missing women associated with Robinson: Izabela Lewicka and Suzette Trouton.

"We ended up finding Suzette's body," Wright said. "She was decomposed by then. You know, you're kind of sad because obviously she's gone but you're elated because you finally got something on this guy."

Following a similar lead across state lines, a Missouri task force searched a storage facility where Robinson rented two garages. It was there that police found three similar drums containing the corpses of Beverly Bonner, Sheila Faith and her daughter. All of the five women were murdered in the same way, with one or two blows to the head from a hammer. This was substantial and overwhelming evidence that Robinson was responsible for the death of these women—and perhaps many more...

Conviction

Just as trying to pin down John Edward Robinson proved a slippery affair, his conviction—or the one he deserved—proved somewhat elusive. In 2002, the state of Kansas sentenced him to death for the murders of Trouten and Lewicka, with life imprisonment for killing Stasi because her murder occurred before Kansas reinstated the death penalty.

Simultaneously, Robinson faced a complex legal dilemma in Missouri. Based on evidence discovered in that state, prosecutors were actively pursuing additional murder charges, yet Robinson's attorneys opposed his extradition because Missouri was more likely to push for capital punishment than Kansas.

Ultimately what the Missouri prosecutor Christ Koster wanted was for Robinson to lead investigators to the missing bodies of Lisa Stasi, Paula Godfrey, and Catherine Clampitt. Robinson refused on the strategy that any of this would lead to his further guilt in Kansas. Koster also faced pressure to offer the plea bargain, as it was unclear which state—or jurisdiction—the murders had occurred.

Robinson remained elusive to the end, and thus the prosecutors were put in the position to reach a compromise because the remains would likely never be found without his cooperation. In 2003, Robinson's carefully composed plea only acknowledged that Koster possessed enough evidence to convict him of five of the women: Godfrey, Clampitt, Bonner, and the Faiths. His statement was a guilty plea, but Robinson remained firm on accepting responsibility and was devoid of

remorse. Despite overwhelming evidence and public outcry, Robinson currently remains on death row in Kansas.

Aftermath

As it may be imagined, a life like the serial killer John Edward Robinson's leaves a swath of destruction that reverberates for all of the lives that he touched. Even for those who are only casually acquainted with the particulars of his case, it serves as a cautionary tale to the depravity of the human soul—or maybe the consequences for someone without one.

Surprisingly, throughout Robinson's whole ordeal and clandestine activities, his wife Nancy and their children remained unaware of his other life. Was his wife in denial, complicit, or simply unaware? For the mindset of Robinson, it's hard to form a solid conclusion on her involvement. In 2005, Nancy Robinson filed for divorce after 41 years of marriage, citing "incompatibility" and "irreconcilable differences."

Robinson's misdeeds with handing off Lisa Stasi's daughter to his brother and sister-in-law caused further pain and suffering. In 2006, Lisa Stasi's daughter (known as Heather Robinson since being illegally adopted) filed a civil suit against Truman Medical Center in Kansas City and against the social worker in charge, Karen Gaddis. Heather Robinson argued that Gaddis informed John Edward Robinson about Stasi and her newborn daughter in 1984; the claim rested on the idea that Gaddis didn't follow up on Robinson's legitimacy after he asked her he was looking for women for his fictitious home for "unwed mothers of white babies." It wasn't until 2007 that Heather Robinson and the hospital reached a settlement for an undisclosed sum, which Heather Robinson agreed to split with her biological grandmother, Patricia Sylvester.

***

While some serial killers tend to follow a sexual deviant's path, Robinson's con artistry added another level of questioning: was he truly a "master" of deviance, or were the mechanisms of the state to weed out individuals of his caliber insufficient? Worse, like his membership to the BDSM cult, were others equally complicit—and are they still among us?

In addition, for all the promise and freedom of the Internet, here was the antithesis, luring those who decided to pursue the more "free" realms of human interaction, only to be preyed upon by someone who had terrible designs for those that wanted to explore their sexual preferences. Nowadays, it seems commonplace to be mistrustful of those we meet online, especially with a whole proliferation of scam artists and predators.

Finally, for those among the sexual community of BDSM, a conviction of this sort casts doubt on the validity and consensual experience of those that choose to be a part of it. Can anyone truly trust one another after a killer like John Edward Robinson flew beneath the radar for so long? These are questions that color the very essence of experience as human beings seeking pleasure and reassurance. This is what a serial killer is truly capable of.

The Internet Black Widow

ANITA MORRISON

Melissa Ann Shepard, also known as the internet black widow, is a cold blooded woman who has regularly been on the wrong side of the law. She was released from jail again in 2016. But, even at 82 years of age, she could still pose a very real threat to any single men that cross her path.

Melissa hasn't always been a danger to men. She was born, Melissa Ann Russell, on the 16th May 1935 in New Brunswick, Canada. Melissa's first marriage, to Russel Shepard, seemed relatively normal. The marriage lasted over two decades, before eventually ending in divorce. Perhaps this experience turned Melissa cynical, because every relationship that followed was anything but normal. Melissa and Shepard had been living in Prince Edward Island for 25 years, although she had served time in jail for fraud. In fact, there were over 30 fraud convictions between 1977 and 1991. Locally, she was thought of as a small town girl who was hungry for wealth, someone who wanted to live the high life. Still, at worst she could be described as a petty criminal. No one would ever have expected what was to follow.

In 1989, Melissa met Gordon Stewart. Stewart was 42 years old and at a vulnerable time in his life. His first wife died in 1986. It had been a successful, loving marriage. Stewart was still grieving the loss several years later, often feeling down and lonely. Having worked in the army for many years, Stewart had savings of around $50000 in the bank, plus a good pension. Gordon Stewart's sister, Kate Reeves, said that she "thought it would be wonderful if he met someone and the sooner the better. But, that feeling lasted a very short time."

When Melissa first met Stewart, she introduced herself as a devout Christian. She seemed very normal and sweet, and quickly gained Stewart's trust. Melissa was actually still married to her first husband at this time, but that didn't stop her. Although supportive at first, Stewart's friends and family started to grow suspicious when stories of her involvement in fraud began to surface. Prince Edward Island is a small place, and it's not easy to keep secrets there. Stewart's brother,

Brian, and sister, Kate Reeves, discovered that Melissa had been in and out of jail, and had used various different names. A local member of the police force even advised them that Gordon Stewart should stay away from Melissa. But, Stewart wouldn't listen. He was smitten.

The new couple married in Las Vegas and she became known as Melissa Ann Stewart. Unfortunately, the honeymoon period didn't last very long. Stewart already had a drinking habit, but it seemed to get progressively worse after he met Melissa. He also ran into some money troubles. His life savings, $50000, were disappearing fast. However, money worries quickly took a back seat when Stewart starting to experience various health problems. Stewart lost a significant amount of weight, and was regularly taken into hospital after passing out and collapsing. Doctors found drugs in his system, as well as copious amounts of alcohol. Some people assumed that he had developed a more serious addiction. However, Brian Stewart was suspicious, he found out that Melissa had access to prescription drugs and he "just knew there was something going on".

The pair seemed to bring out the worst in each other, and one night a fight broke out over money. Melissa claimed that Stewart hit her, and he served jail time for this alleged attack. Stewart's family were shocked by this and Kate Reeves claimed that "this is not an abused wife... this was an abusive, is an abusive, person herself". After spending time in jail, Stewart was released on the condition that he stayed away from Melissa. However, Melissa initiated contact again, saying that she wanted to work on their marriage.

In the early spring of 1991, the couple moved to Halifax. Stewart had agreed that a change of scenery might help their troubled marriage. Sadly, this wasn't to be. After only one week in Halifax, they set off on a weekend drive from which only one would return.

The couple drove to a secluded area. Later toxicology reports showed that Stewart had a lethal amount of alcohol and prescription drugs in his system, and experts believed that he would have been unable to function. However, Melissa claimed that another argument broke out, again about money. She alleged that, following the argument, Stewart attacked and raped her. In order to escape from him, she jumped back into the car and tried to drive away. Apparently, she accidentally reversed over her husband, thinking he was a log. She then accelerated over him again, and drove off quickly. Two people witnessed the horrific events, and watched as Melissa left the scene. Gordon Stewart was dead.

Melissa drove to a police station, and told them that she wanted to report a rape. Almost as an afterthought, she added that she had killed the perpetrator – her husband. According to police, this immediately aroused suspicion. Why wouldn't she have remained at the scene to explain her story? Suspicion grew when it was discovered that there was no evidence of rape, or any kind of attack on Melissa, and toxicology reports showed that it was unlikely Stewart was even conscious at the time. The outcome of the investigation was that Melissa's motive for killing Stewart had been monetary, not in self-defence. Stewart had a large pension and, as his wife, Melissa would have been eligible for various benefits. Despite the evidence stacked up against her, Melissa told a compelling story in court, painting a picture of a violent marriage and a battered woman. She was convicted only of manslaughter, and was given a six year sentence.

Before she had even been released from jail, Melissa started to use the situation to her advantage. She became a poster girl for women's rights and starred in a major documentary about escaping abusive marriages. Unbelievably, she was released after serving only two years in prison, this was put down to good behaviour, but probably had something to do with her new found fame. After her release in 1994, she began to make many public appearances. Melissa claimed that "no one knew I was a battered woman", and she encouraged others in similar circumstances to speak out and get help. She became a very well-known figure in the media throughout the 1990s. Popular opinion, influenced by Melissa's emotionally charged story, was that the killing of Stewart was a heroic act.

Towards the end of the 1990s, Melissa decided that she wanted a fresh start. She moved to Florida, and began attending a local Church. That was where, in the year 2000, she met Robert Friedrich.

Robert Friedrich was another vulnerable man, whose wife of 53 years had died in 1999. When he met Melissa, he was 82. In his younger years, Friedrich had been a very successful engineer and inventor. His life savings were estimated to be around $300000, he also owned his house, and had several insurance policies. Friedrich had sons, but they lived quite far away in Boston. Friedrich was lonely, and had been struggling to cope with the loss of his beloved wife. Melissa claimed that when she saw Friedrich at Church, the Holy Spirit spoke to her and told her that he would be her next husband. Only three days after meeting, Melissa and Friedrich were engaged.

Friedrich's family were concerned. His son, Dennis, and daughter in law, Karen, say that at first they were cautiously optimistic, thinking perhaps it would be good for Friedrich to have some company. However, when marriage was mentioned so quickly, it set off alarm bells. Friedrich wanted his son's approval to marry Melissa, but Dennis refused to give it. His main concern was that she could be a gold digger. In the end, the outcome was much worse.

Despite his family encouraging him not to rush, Friedrich married Melissa having known her for less than one month. Melissa acquired another name, Melissa Ann Friedrich. The wedding took place in secret, in Dartmouth, Nova Scotia. Dennis Friedrich was very angry with his father, but there was little he could do other than cross his fingers and hope that the marriage would be a happy one.

The newlyweds set off on the honeymoon of a lifetime, which lasted for five months and significantly decreased Friedrich's life savings. On their return, they settled in Bradenton, Florida. According to family members, Friedrich seemed content. Even at 82, he had always been in good health, but after returning to Florida this quickly began to change. He became unsteady on his feet, and fell over several times. A worrying pattern started to emerge. Friedrich would feel dizzy, fall, and end up in hospital. He would then recover quickly and be sent home, only for the same thing to happen again a few days later. Friedrich's son Dennis also noticed that his father often seemed confused on the phone, slurring his words, and not sounding his normal self. Suspicions grew when Friedrich visited Dennis in Boston, and appeared totally fine, almost back to his old self again. Dennis realised that Friedrich only got ill when Melissa was around. The family decided that something needed to be done. Friedrich's other son, Bob, contacted an Elder Abuse Agency in Florida. The agency visited Friedrich at home, and recommended that he should have 24 hour care, to ensure that he was being looked after properly. Melissa refused this care, and even threatened to sue the agency involved. She left a threatening voice mail message for Friedrich's sons, saying that they were being cut out of Friedrich's will and would be left with nothing: "you guys are getting nothing, a big fat zero".

After being married for less than 18 months, in December 2002, Robert Friedrich died of a heart attack. As his wife, Melissa was responsible for making the necessary arrangements following the death. Dennis claims that the doctor who signed the death certificate for Friedrich didn't even see his body in person; he simply took Melissa's word for it over the phone. Melissa organized for Friedrich's body to be cremated extremely quickly after his death, meaning that there was never a chance to conduct an autopsy. Melissa stayed in Florida for about five months. During which time she sold the house and collected various insurance payments, pocketing around $100000. Friedrich's family were left with nothing but sad memories, and pictures.

By 2004, Melissa was back in Prince Edward Island and moving on with her life. But Friedrich's son Dennis was haunted by his father's death. He would regularly type Melissa's name into Google, even trying other names that he knew she had used previously, Melissa Ann Russell, Melissa Ann Shepard, and Melissa Ann Stewart. Finally, he found an article in the Halifax Herald called "Too Many Deaths along Old Guysborough Road". The article covered the killing of Gordon Stewart and Melissa's strange history. At that point, Dennis Friedrich was in little doubt about what was behind his father's fast decline. Dennis is still convinced that Robert Friedrich was poisoned by Melissa. He tried to make a criminal case against her, but it was impossible because no evidence of the crime remained. Dennis has stated that Melissa is "not just a gold digger, she's a murderer".

Melissa has always denied killing Friedrich, claiming that marriage was a very good one and she wouldn't have had any reason to want him dead. She said that she has been "railroaded" and misunderstood, and that these strange happenings were merely coincidences.

During 2004, Melissa was living happily off Friedrich's $100000. But, it turned out that this wasn't her only source of income. Melissa had also been claiming spousal benefits under the names Shepard and Stewart and using different social security numbers. When police discovered this, they set out to arrest her. But, she was gone. By November 2004, Melissa had started travelling back to Florida again, to meet yet another potential victim.

Alex Strategos was 73 years old and lived in Pinellas Park, Florida. He had two previous unsuccessful marriages, and had been living alone for 10 years. Alex Strategos moved to Florida in 2002 to be closer to his son, Dean. Strategos had developed some health problems; he was diabetic and experienced a stroke. Despite the health issues, Strategos was happy in Florida. Family friend Judi Frock said that he seemed fine, but wasn't very talkative, spending a lot of time on the computer. Judi Frock and Dean Strategos both wanted him to meet someone, they didn't realise that he already had- over the internet.

Melissa first contacted Alex Strategos on the 6th of October 2004, she saw his profile on a Christian dating website, and sent him a message. They discussed how she had used to live very close to Strategos' home, but that she had moved back to Prince Edward Island after becoming widowed. After less than four weeks of messaging, Melissa suggested a visit. She said that she would drive down to Florida from Canada, around 2000 miles. Strategos asked where she was planning to stay; he warned her that he only had one bedroom. Melissa wasn't fazed by this. In fact, she seemed very keen.

When Strategos mentioned the upcoming visit to his son Dean and family friend, Judi Frock, they were very surprised. They both thought it was a little strange that a woman would be willing to drive so far alone and stay with someone on the first meeting. However, they were happy that Strategos had met someone, and wanted to be supportive. Melissa made the long drive down to Florida.

On her arrival, Melissa and Strategos went out for a long, romantic meal. After they had finished dining, they returned to his condo. Melissa opened a bottle of wine and brought Strategos a glass. When it got late, Strategos offered to sleep on the couch, but Melissa refused this, saying that she wanted to sleep with him. During the night, Alex Strategos woke up feeling unwell. He tried to make his way to the bathroom, but was overcome with dizziness and passed out. Strategos had no idea that this mysterious illness had proved very common among Melissa's previous husbands too.

Alex Strategos was admitted to hospital on the night of his first meeting with Melissa. She told hospital staff that she was his wife. She also took his house keys, saying that she would keep the place nice for him. With Strategos still in the hospital, Melissa went back to his house and made herself at home. Dean Strategos visited Melissa at the house, saying that his father had sent him to see how she was doing. Melissa was surprised; she hadn't known that Strategos had a son. The first impression that Dean Strategos got was that she seemed nice -

classy and polite. Dean had been worried that Melissa was just after his father's money. But, after their first meeting and seeing Melissa's white Cadillac, his fears subsided. It seemed like she had plenty of money of her own, so why would she need to steal any from Alex Strategos?

After a few days in hospital, Strategos seemed to recover. Doctors couldn't find a reason for his collapse, so they sent him home. Melissa promised to care for him and she appeared to be doing a good job. The house was always kept spotless, and Strategos said that she was an excellent cook. Dean Strategos and Judi Frock visited the couple, and found a very pleasant scene. Everything seemed to be working out fine. Alex Strategos started to talk about marriage, even though he had only known Melissa for a couple of months.

Less than a week passed before Strategos was admitted to hospital again, and a familiar pattern emerged. Over the following two months, Alex Strategos was rushed to hospital a further seven times. Dean was worried about his father's health. But, initially he didn't suspect Melissa, he was actually glad that she was there keeping an eye on Alex. It was family friend, Judi Frock, who had doubts. She thought the whole situation was very odd, and noticed that Alex Strategos always got more ill when he was around Melissa. She mentioned this to her work colleagues, one of whom was the wife of a local police officer. Frock's colleague called her husband, Mike Lynch, and told him what had been going on. The story raised several red flags for Lynch, and he decided to look into it further.

Meanwhile, nurses moved Strategos into a 24 hour nursing home, so that he could be monitored properly. Melissa lied to nurses at the home, saying that she was Strategos' wife. She then tried to get him a permanent place at the home, without consulting either Alex Strategos himself, or his son Dean. A nurse told Dean this information, along with the shocking revelation that Melissa had also made Strategos sign a power of attorney document whilst he was very ill. Melissa was now in control of all Strategos' property and finances. This alarmed Dean, and he realised that something was very wrong.

Mike Lynch began his investigation by talking to Alex Strategos. Strategos told Lynch that he couldn't remember any of the times he had passed out, this felt very different to any medical problems he had previously experienced. Initially, Strategos didn't want to believe that Melissa could be behind his illness, until Lynch looked at his blood work and found something very strange. There were relatively high levels of benzodiazepine, a powerful tranquilizer, in Strategos' blood. Strategos had never been prescribed sedatives. Mike Lynch had seen benzodiazepine being used as a recreational drug, so he knew what the effects were – dizziness, confusion, and collapsing. Strategos told Lynch that every night before bed Melissa would bring him a small bowl of his favourite ice cream. Lynch believed that this was how Melissa was getting him to ingest the drug.

The next move was to look for a motive, and Lynch found one quickly. Melissa had made several large bank transfers from Strategos' account to her own. Overall, there was around $18000 missing. Dean and Alex Strategos were both horrified when they heard this news. There was no doubt left in their minds that Melissa was up to no good. After further investigation they discovered Melissa's other names, and her dark past. The police arrested her, and found a large stash of benzodiazepine and other prescription drugs in her possession. Luckily for Melissa, they couldn't prosecute her for attempted murder because the levels of benzodiazepine in Strategos' blood were not high enough to kill him. Instead, she was convicted of several charges including exploiting the elderly, forgery, and theft. She was sentenced to five years in jail. Melissa denies any wrong doing, maintaining that the missing money was used on Strategos' request to pay bills and look after the house. Alex Strategos described Melissa as "cold-blooded", saying that she tricked and deceived him. Dean made up the name the "internet black widow", a name that has stuck, and with good reason.

Melissa was released in 2009, a year early. Eventually, she headed back to Canada and moved into a retirement complex near New Glasgow. Melissa had family connections in the area. People assumed that as a relatively elderly lady, Melissa's black widow days would be over. But, this proved to be far from the truth. In September 2012, a man named Fred Weeks received a visit from a neighbour, who introduced herself as Millie Ann Russell.

Fred Weeks was another widower, 75 years of age. In his working days he had been a teacher, and was described as a very kind man. Weeks and Melissa shared a whirlwind romance, and they married on the 25th September 2012 in New Glasgow, just two weeks after they first met. The marriage was conducted by an old friend of Weeks, Justice of the Peace, George Megeney. Megeney said that "they were happy at that time, or at least Fred was, and Millie appeared to be". However, the Justice of the Peace began to have serious doubts about Millie after a friend recognised her, and revealed her former identity. George Megeney contacted the police, but as no crime had been committed, they were powerless to act.

Weeks and Melissa went on a short honeymoon to Newfoundland. They were there for four days, before heading to North Sydney, a ferry terminal town on the route back to New Glasgow. When booking a room at a bed and breakfast, Melissa informed the owner, Cheryl Chambers, that they were both a little travel sick and needed to rest. Cheryl Chambers noticed that "Mr Weeks didn't look well at all", describing his appearance as gaunt. Whereas Mrs Weeks, Melissa, looked healthy, well-groomed even, in a red suit. This struck Chambers as odd, and she decided to keep an eye on the elderly couple. Later that evening she knocked on the door to check on them. Melissa answered and told her that everything was fine, they were just resting. Chambers could see Mr Weeks on the bed, still looking very ill, she was concerned.

In the morning, Chambers asked Melissa if there had been any improvement in Mr Weeks' condition. When she heard that the answer was no, she offered to call an ambulance. Melissa said yes, but that she would like to finish eating her breakfast and get ready first. This alarmed Chambers, who called an ambulance immediately. Fred Weeks was taken to hospital, where Melissa informed the doctor that he had no children and that he had been prescribed tranquilizers – these statements were of course false. Luckily, the hospital staff had access to his medical records, and realised that she was lying. They called the police. Melissa had already made her way back home to New Glasgow. People began to make the connection, news spread and the media debated the possibility that the internet black widow had struck again.

Melissa was charged with attempted murder, but again the charge didn't stick. Even though police knew how dangerous Melissa was, they couldn't prosecute her without sufficient evidence. The judge accepted her guilty plea for failing to provide the necessities of life and administering a noxious substance. In 2013, the 78 year old was sentenced to three and a half years in jail.

Luckily, Fred Weeks recovered. He understood that it was all lies and that Melissa had tried to kill him. "She was good at it, got to give her that" remarked Weeks.

On the 18th of March 2016, a white haired Melissa was released from prison. The terms for her release included not being allowed any access to the internet whatsoever, and having to inform the police if she started any romantic relationships, so that the man in question could be warned about her history.

Less than one month later, on the 11th of April 2016, Melissa was spotted by a community police officer at Halifax Central Library. The officer approached, and discovered that Melissa was accessing the internet. He also found a device in her possession that could be used to get online. These were breaches of Melissa's release conditions, so she was arrested again. On the 4th of August 2016, her lawyers entered not guilty pleas for all the charges, with her trial set to take place early 2017. However, on the 22nd of December 2016, all charges against Melissa were dropped.

Melissa's luck seems to be never ending. Despite having had a hand in two deaths, and poisoning a further two men, she has spent a surprisingly short amount of time in jail. Chief Justice Joseph Philip Kennedy advised that "people who have contact with this lady should be very careful". There is no reason to believe that Melissa has changed her ways, in fact the opposite is likely. Single, elderly men beware; the internet black widow is still on the hunt.

WENDI ANDRIANO

MICHELLE TYSON

Chapter 1

A dying husband needs a devoted wife. But when love runs out, marriage becomes a burden.

On October 8, 2000, Wendi Andriano snapped. She had played the part of devoted wife to her terminally ill husband, Joe Andriano, for years, but when the love left their marriage, so did Wendi's patience for her husband's eventual demise.

Wendi had a plan to help nudge nature along, and when her plan b expired, she took matters directly into her own hands and bludgeoned him to death.

Wendi first tried to poison her husband by spiking his last meal, a homemade beef stew, with sodium azide, but Joe Andriano did not ingest enough to kill him, only enough to vomit it back up. Wendi then grabbed the nearest object, a bar stool, and beat her dying husband over the head so many times that parts of his brain became exposed.

After thinking she had successfully killed her husband twice, Wendi then realized that Joe was still breathing, so she took a knife from the family kitchen and stabbed him in the side of the throat.

Minutes later, Joe was finally dead.

This bizarre and frantic way Wendi killed her husband isn't the strangest thing about the case though. Known even to Wendi, Joe was due to die from terminal cancer within the next few years anyways.

Why Wendi couldn't wait to kill her husband is an intriguing tale wrought with sex, lies, and strangely, a lack of patience.

Chapter 2

Wendi and Joe Andriano grew up together in the small farming community of Casa Grande, Arizona. But while they both had gone to the same school, they never dated. As a minister's daughter, Wendi's social life was restricted to her father's church. Her celebration for graduating high school was even in the form of a missionary trip to Mexico in 1989. When she returned she took a job at the local clerical hospital.

Wendi met Joe in 1992 through friends. Although when the couple started dating Joe's family found the minister's daughter to be an unusual fit for the loud, outgoing former football player, they all thought she was friendly enough and approved of the match.

Joe worked for a local boat builder. He was very mechanically inclined and was a very good welder. He owned his own boat and took Wendi for several cruises around the local hot spots for speedboats. They were inseparable.

The couple married in January of 1994. Their wedding took place in a baptist church across the street from their shared elementary school. Their reception was at the Elk's club and was populated by their many friends and family. Even after two years of dating, though, Joe's family felt like they didn't know his new bride very well, but Joe seemed to be very happy, so they were happy for him.

Soon after marrying, the couple became business partners when they started a small company that did windshield repair and replacement. The business combined Wendi's office experience with Joe's mechanical experience, skills they both exceeded at, and the business thrived.

The couple hadn't been married a whole year yet before they faced their first major challenge together. That fall, Joe noticed an odd bump on his neck. When he had it tested, he was told it was a non-cancerous benign tumor, but it wasn't long before they were second-guessing the diagnoses. A year after it was removed, the tumor grew back.

A second surgery and round of tests seemed to reconfirm that the tumor was benign, but shortly after Wendi gave birth to a son in 1997, the tumor was back yet again.

The third time the tumor returned, Joe's wife and family were convinced that the tumor had to be cancer. This fear was confirmed in 1998 when Joe underwent surgery to have the bump removed for the fourth time. Joe's pre-surgery chest x-ray showed that not only was the tumor cancerous, but that the cancer had now spread across Joe's throat, chest, and lungs.

The prognosis wasn't good—Joe had a rare form of cancer and while radiation and chemotherapy were standard, there was no guarantee they would work. On top of this, Wendi was also pregnant again and was only months away from giving birth to the couple's second child.

Chapter 3

In an effort to increase Joe's chances of survival while decreasing his suffering, Wendi and Joe decided to pursue holistic treatments before resorting to chemotherapy and radiation. They had been told that chemotherapy and radiation treatments would likely not cure Joe, but they would lengthen his life by a few years; however, these years would be anything from pleasant. The horrific side-effects chemotherapy and radiation treatments cause are well known.

So the Andriano's decided first to try anything from special diets to alternative medical treatments to prayer—anything that had a chance to help Joe. Joe even attended a holistic treatment centre for cancer patients in Colorado for a few weeks where he was surrounded by other men and women facing the same prognosis as him. After seeing the bravery of others in the same position as him, Joe began thinking about his future again and began to see it as bright for the first time in a while.

After Joe returned from his holistic healing getaway with a bright new attitude, the Andriano's decided the next best step would be for Joe to begin chemotherapy treatments. He had begun to crave his future and was ready to take steps to achieve it. Unfortunately, taking these steps meant that Joe needed to quit his welding job as well as his own position in the couple's business.

To help make ends meet, Wendi returned to working for the first time since the birth of the couple's children. She ended up taking multiple jobs and worked long hours while continuing to care for her husband at home. Eventually, Wendi landed a job managing the San

Riva apartment complex in the Ahwatukee foothills, an upscale neighbourhood outside of Phoenix.

Wendi's new job came with some major perks—the salary was above average, which was nice as Wendi was now the family's breadwinner, and it required Wendi to live on site, which meant that the family now lived in a luxury apartment but paid no rent. Wendi's new job also gave her a new life. A large part of her duties as complex manager was arranging social activities for the other residents of the San Riva apartments, who were mostly young, wealthy, single businesspeople.

Every Saturday the complex hosted picnics, pool parties, or late-night socials. The residents even had their own baseball team. Wendi was required to attend every event, which meant Joe was needed to stay home with their two children. Wendi enjoyed this alone time so much that many of the residents at the San Riva had no clue she had a dying husband and two children at home. She partied like she was single.

The first few months at the San Riva went well. Wendi organized mixers and pool parties for the tenants while Joe took care of the kids. Despite being very weak from treatments, he did everything he could, he wanted to do it. He prefered to have his kids around him even when he didn't feel good.

Although they had never gotten close to their daughter-in-law, Joe's parents also pitched in with babysitting so the couple could have time alone together. They didn't get to see each other much as Wendi began spending more and more time at work. Her new job had also given her a new confidence, and she spent many nights out on the town dancing and drinking away her weekday stress with friends. Joe began to fear that Wendi would soon leave him for her new lifestyle, but this fear got sidetracked when his health continued to fail.

In the summer of 2000, when tests revealed his cancer had spread yet again, Joe and Wendi decided to increase the frequency of Joe's chemotherapy. Joe agreed to undergo more treatments, but they quickly took their toll. He lost 15 pounds in the first week alone, and Joe's doctor became concerned. It went from bad to worse very quickly.

By the beginning of October 2000, it became harder and harder to remain optimistic about Joe's chances of beating his cancer. It became apparent it was terminal, but doctors insisted that with treatment Joe could live for several more years.

No one had any idea that Joe would be dead after only the first week of the month. No one, that is, except for one person—Wendi Andriano.

Chapter 4

Just after 2:00 a.m. on October 8, Wendi Andriano called a friend who also lived in the San Riva apartment complex. She told her friend that she needed someone to stay with the kids while she took Joe to the hospital. When the friend arrived, she found Joe on the floor, barely alive.

Joe was on the floor in the fetal position. There was vomit on the floor around him and he couldn't stand up. Wendi confided in her friend that she told Joe that she had called 9-1-1 and paramedics were on the way, but this wasn't true. After seeing Joe in such poor condition, the neighbour urged Wendi to call paramedics. She then went outside to wait for them to arrive while Wendi waiting with her husband.

Wendi did call 9-1-1, but when the EMT's arrived minutes later, she refused to let them or her friend inside the apartment. She said that her husband was dying from terminal cancer and had a do not resuscitate order. Joe was not to receive any medical attention.

Just over an hour later, at 3:30 a.m., Wendi dialed 9-1-1 a second time. The same team of paramedics came to the house. It didn't take them long to realize something wasn't quite right, so they contacted the police department. Both the paramedics and the police were shocked to find out that Joe, who had been terminally ill from cancer for quite some time had died, but not from the cancer that had been slowly killing his body. He died from being repeatedly beaten with a bar stool and from being stabbed in the neck.

When the police opened the front door of the apartment, they were confronted with obvious signs of a deadly struggle. The apartment was in a complete state of disarray, and there was blood everywhere. Blood had been traced throughout the kitchen, the dining room, and the living room of the luxury apartment, and blood had spattered across the walls the ceilings. Lying in the middle of the bloody scene was Joe, with a knife wound in his neck and holes spattered across his visible skull.

While crime scene technicians surveyed the apartment, phoenix police took Wendi down to the station for a formal statement. She was wearing clothes drenched in Joe's blood and was armed with a story that explained how Joe's death had been a complete accident.

In the interrogation room, Wendi told police she and joe had spent the evening in Casa Grande visiting with Joe's parents. They put the kids to bed after they returned home, which was when Joe noticed something odd about Wendi's appearance—she wasn't wearing her wedding ring.

According to Wendi, Joe worked himself into a rage and began accusing her of having an affair. This argument turned into a shoving match, and when Joe grabbed a belt, Wendi grabbed a bar stool and swung. Joe went down on all fours so she hit him again. It was then that she called her neighbour for help. Joe may have been in a terrible state when the neighbour saw him, but according to Wendi when she went outside Joe had gotten back to his feet easily.

Wendi said she denied the EMTs access to the apartment because she and Joe were both embarrassed about the fight, but just minutes after the EMTs left, the fight got physical again.

Wendi said that her husband tried to strangle her with a telephone cord and she defended herself with the first weapon she could get in her hands—a kitchen knife. She was vague about how the knife ended up in Joe's neck though, saying she was holding the knife up when Joe suddenly fell flat on his face. The next thing she knew, blood was spurting everywhere. He must have fallen on the blade, it was simply an accident.

Many things about this story didn't make sense to the police. First of all, the timeline presented in Wendi's story didn't match the accounts of Wendi's neighbour or the EMTs. Wendi's neighbour had seen no evidence of a physical fight when they first entered the apartment—there were no broken bar stools or blood like later when the police arrived. As well, Wendi had few injuries on her body, definitely no injuries that would necessitate self defence in the form of murder.

Joe's illness also shed doubt on Wendi's story. Joe's parents told police that when the Andriano's visited earlier that evening, Joe had been so weak from his treatments that he could barely stand. They had spent the evening doting on their sick son, bringing him any comforts he wanted. If he was too weak to stand, he certainly couldn't have been strong enough to violently attack Wendi.

Police also uncovered a damning piece of evidence from Wendi herself, in a moment when she thought she was all alone. The investigators that had been questioning Wendi left her on her own in the interrogation room for some time while they fact checked some of her statements and checked in with the investigators who were scanning the crime scene for evidence. During this time, Wendi made a phone call to a coworker at the apartment complex and asked them to hide some of her files from the police. This immediately led to a search of Wendi's office where police found evidence that Wendi had in fact killed her husband. She had even been planning it for months.

Chapter 5

While both investigators strongly believed that Wendi Andriano was responsible for Joe's death, they were stumped by her motive. Why would Wendi kill her dying husband? The police didn't know, but they did have one intriguing lead—the phone call Wendi had made from the interrogation room. They were determined to find out what she was trying to hide.

When they searched her office, police discovered that Wendi had been disciplined at work for using her computer to search inappropriate items on the internet while on the clock.She had been conducting research on poisons, and how to use certain poisons to kill people. They also discovered the papers that she had tried to hide—shipping notices for a substance known as sodium azide.

Sodium azide is a lethal substance with a variety of industrial uses including propelling airbags. It is not, however, something that the average person can simply go out and buy. It's not restricted to the point where only certain companies can possess it, but it needs to be bought for a reason—something that an apartment complex didn't have. But based on the information on the shipping invoice, Wendi had found a way around that.

Wendi had created a fictitious business license using the tax ID form for the apartment complex. Using a Xerox machine and an exacto knife, Wendi had removed all information specific to the apartment complex and inserted fictitious information for a fake company.

The business name on the shipping notice was bogus, but the address wasn't. Wendi had the substance delivered to an address in Scottsdale, Arizona in an attempt to distance herself, but that plan didn't work. When the police tracked down the real address on the invoice, workers at the company positively identified Wendi as the person who had come by a couple weeks earlier to pick up a package she had mistakenly had shipped there instead of her own office.

Wendi's coworkers had seen her with a package but that she had been very mysterious with the contents. She refused to tell anyone what was inside. Had this been the sodium azide? And if so, where was it now?

Chapter 6

Suspecting that Wendi had tried to poison Joe with the sodium azide, police took samples of every medication and food they could find in the Andriano's apartment. If Joe had ingested poison, it would have explained the awful state Wendi's friend had seen him in just over an hour before he died. Luckily, the remainders of Joe's last supper, homemade beef stew, still sat in a pot on the stove.

However, police didn't find any evidence of Wendi's mysterious package, or any evidence of the sodium azide itself in Wendi and Joe's apartment. They had just begun to lose hope in finding the poison when they found out Wendi had a storage space in the building that she failed to tell the police about. Hidden behind a stack of boxes in Wendi's storage unit was a small bottle of white powder and a measuring spoon. The white powder was soon identified as sodium azide.

But the storage unit wasn't the only place investigators found the lethal substance—it was also in Joe's stomach contents and in the beef stew on the stove.

While discovering the poison helped police understand that Wendi had been trying to kill her husband, it didn't explain why she had bludgeoned him to death on October 8, 2000. Wendi had spent a lot of time researching poisons and she spent a lot of time manufacturing documents so that she could purchase the poison. It certainly wasn't a spur of the moment decision.

But why would Wendi beat and stab her husband if she had already poisoned him? Prosecutors had a theory, one that would cut to the heart of the crime. It was patience—or more precisely, Wendi's lack of it—that had killed Joe in the end.

Wendi had grown tired of waiting for the cancer to kill Joe, so she decided to give nature a little nudge by poisoning his supper. But according to the theory, when Wendi gave Joe the poison, things didn't go quite to plan. Joe hadn't ingested enough poison to kill him when he began vomiting it back up. With her plan quickly failing, Wendi panicked. She snapped.

Now improvising, Wendi beat Joe with the nearest object she could get her hands on—a bar stool. Pathologists were able to conclude that Wendi beat Joe over the head with the stool no less than twenty-four times. This beating did render Joe unconscious, but still didn't kill him so Wendi grabbed a kitchen knife and stabbed him in the part of his body that caused all this trouble in the first place—the side of his neck.

Chapter 7

Ten days after she murdered her husband, Wendi Andriano was formally charged with first degree murder. Wendi's crime was viewed as being especially cruel due to the large amount of suffering Joe had had to endure over several hours thanks to Wendi's actions. Because of this, the prosecutor's on Wendi's trial did the almost unthinkable, they sought the death penalty.

When Wendi a walked into the Arizona courtroom on September 9, 2004 she looked vastly different from the perky apartment manager that the residents of the San Riva apartments used to know.

At the time of the killing she had been blonde, she had short hair, and generally appeared to be much younger and cute than the individual who appeared in court with long dark hair and thick glasses. Previously, she had liked to look good and show her figure so her conservative dress at the trial was certainly different from the look her friends were used to seeing. She was trying to look more conservative, more innocent.

She had had plenty of time to perfect her new look—it had taken prosecutors almost four years to bring the case to trial. It had been postponed about 12 times before it was finally brought before a judge and jury.

In their opening statement, prosecutors reminded the jury that at the time of the murder Wendi had been anything but the perfect mother or wife she claimed to have been. She had been someone who had no disregard for her husband at all. While her husband was dying, she had gone out partying and started affairs, and when his condition worsened, and it began to cramp her style, she turned to poison.

Wendi didn't like her new role as family breadwinner, especially with the loss of Joe's income, and with rising medical bills, the family was in the worst financial state they had ever been in. Wendi had thought she was going to be able to be a stay-at-home-mom for the rest of her life, and she did not adjust well to her return to the workforce. So Wendi had found an out.

Although Joe did not have any life insurance, even though Wendi had asked several friends to pretend to be Joe in medical exams so he could be insured, Joe had filed a malpractice suit against his former doctor who had continually told him his tumor was benign when it was in fact spreading throughout his body. If Joe died and the lawsuit went through, Wendi would likely walk away with a multi-million dollar settlement.

More than money though, Wendi had wanted freedom. She wanted the freedom to be single again, she wanted freedom to the ball-and-chain who was slowly dragging her spirit into his grave along with himself. Wendi wanted to not have to care about her dying husband anymore, who was too weak to provide her with any love.

Wendi maintained her plea of innocence throughout the trial, and her defence team attempted to prove she had been the victim of abuse not only on the night of Joe's death but also throughout the couple's entire marriage. To explain the poison, Wendi told the court that Joe had been the one who had grown tired of waiting for the cancer to end his life, and had asked Wendi to help him do it himself.

On the witness stand Wendi said that Joe had willingly taken the poison, but she also stuck by the story that she had originally told police, that Joe had suspected an affair and became enraged when she affirmed them. He became deranged and attacked her, starting the bloody fight. Wendi claimed Joe had died during the ensuing struggle.

Wendi's story wasn't enough to convince the court though, and on November 18, 2004 she was found guilty of the crime. It had taken the jury only two-and-a-half-hours to come to its unanimous decision. Six years after her husband joe had been diagnosed with terminal cancer, Wendi Andriano faced a possible death sentence of her own.

On December 20, 2004, the jurors assigned to Wendi Andriano's case met and decided on Wendi's fate—it would be death for Ms Andriano. Wendi, along with most of the courtroom, was aghast. Even Joe's family was shocked by the decision. Wendi Andriano became the second ever woman to be put on death row in Arizona, a state that reserves the death penalty for the worst of the worst.

Wendi Andriano has since attempted to appeal the court's decision, but as of early 2017, all attempts have been denied and Wendi continues to wait on death row. Wendi and Joe's children now live with Joe's parents, who continue to mourn the loss of their beloved son.

Joe Andriano's death was especially long, and especially cruel, but no happy ending was found when Wendi was sentenced to her own death. Many view the conclusion of this case to be the saddest possible outcome. On October 8, 2000, two lives were lost, and two children were left without parents.

A DEADLY INTERNET LOVE TRIANGLE

59

MICHELLE BLUE

Chapter 1

Sharee Miller was a gorgeous, single mother-of-three when she met her husband Bruce Miller. At the time, she was in her early twenties, broke, and weeks away from being homeless.

The couple initially met when Sharee began working at Bruce's automobile scrap yard as a bookkeeper. After only three months, Sharee moved herself and her three kids into Bruce's house and they quickly became a family. Bruce gave Sharee a sense of stability she had never experienced and Sharee was kind, caring, and loving to Bruce.

After only a few more months, the couple married. Domestic bliss loomed on the horizon.

But six months later, Bruce was dead.

Initially, the events that led to Bruce's death were a complete mystery to police until a former homicide detective miles away shot himself in the head and left behind a briefcase of evidence.

How these two deaths were connected would shock police, and lead to one of the most infamous crimes in America.

Chapter 2

Sharee Miller, then Sharee Kitley, was born on October 13, 1971, in Flint, Michigan.

At the time, Flint was a powerhouse of economic growth largely due to the GM Buick and Chevrolet factories that operated in the city. General Motor's history was largely intertwined with Flint—the company's founder had formed the GM company in Flint in 1908. The GM factories in Flint were also the setting of the and iconic 1936-37 Sit-Down Strike—the strike that led to the creation of the United Auto Worker's union.

Flint made money because Flint made cars.

However, the Kitley family did not drink from the city's pool of wealth. They lived on the town's outskirts, a rough working-class neighborhood. They're home was a single-wide trailer smack-dab in the center of a tornado's playground. Sharee was an only child, she was the sole receiver of her parent's attention, but this attention was not desired by Sharee. Sharee's parents fought often, and when they were finished fighting with each other, they'd fight with Sharee.

In mid 80's, when Sharee was in her early teens, GM Motors closed its factories' doors in Flint. The city quickly fell to pieces, ramshackle remains of the auto empire it had once been. The city fell into a deep depression.

As she watched her hometown descend into ruins, Sharee decided to leave her toxic home for good. At the age of 16, Sharee moved in with her boyfriend at the time, and when that ended she couched surfed and work a variety of dead-end jobs, most of which only lasted a few months.

When she was 18, Sharee found herself pregnant and married to an abusive husband. The two shared a home in yet another low-income project in another rough neighborhood left in the dust of Flint's ruined automobile empire. Sharee watched her childhood repeat itself in front of her own eyes, but this time, it was her first-born son who held the starring role of the helpless child. Sharee ended the marriage after she caught her spouse physically abusing the young boy. It was one of the only lines Sharee drew in the sand—you did not harm her children.

Although Sharee took this brave step towards saving her son, history often repeated itself throughout her life. Two more failed attempts at finding a soulmate yielded two more children for the young woman. The single mother-of-three now resorted to frequently moving from low-income house to low-income house and took any odd job she could find—anything to keep her kids off the street.

Chapter 3

In 1997, Sharee was a single mother-of-three who was three breaths and an electricity bill away from being homeless. During an attempt to keep her kids safe and housed, Sharee took a job as a bookkeeper with B&D Auto, a small auto scrapyard that fit right in in the middle of Flint's automobile history.

Sharee had been hired despite having little-to-no experience keeping books in the past. She had convinced the boss, Bruce Miller, that she was hard-working, a fast learner, and desperate for a paycheque. And that seemed to be enough. That and the fact that Sharee was a stunner. Her bright blonde hair only drew more attention to her enrapturing icy blue eyes.

Bruce was a kind and generous soul. He took a chance on Sharee and it seemed to pay off. Only a few months after Sharee had begun working at the scrapyard, she and Bruce moved their relationship from the office to the bedroom. It wasn't long before Sharee and her three kids moved in with Bruce. The four now lived in a stable, secure home for the first time in any of their lives.

Bruce and Sharee married only months after they first met. Bruce, who has twenty-one his new bride's senior, thought he had finally found the perfect wife. Young, sexy, and loving. It was all he had ever wanted.

Her new life with Bruce was also a dream come true for Sharee. She had finally found a man that treated her right, and in him, she also found security. Ten years ago, she had left her own unhappy parents and embarked on a life of poverty and abuse. Now, she was sitting in the living room of a big house, watching her children—the true loves of her life—swimming in Bruce's above-ground pool. It was the idyllic life she never thought she could have.

But idyllicism did not suit Sharee.

Chapter 4

While Sharee lived the life she had always wanted for herself and her kids, Bruce's own family began to have doubts behind Sharee's motives.

Initially, Bruce's family took no issue with the fact that Bruce's wife was so young. The couple looked so happy and in love, they formed a perfect family. Bruce was even in the process of adopting Sharee's three boys. But things slowly began to change.

Sharee began to take advantage of her new wealth. She no longer worked at the scrapyard but began selling Mary Kay Cosmetics to other bored housewives instead. She began spending every penny of her earnings, and a whole lot more of Bruce's, on luxuries she had never been presented with before. She bought expensive jewelry and clothes, she got her first credit card plus a few more, and she bought an expensive computer for the home.

Bruce, however, did not partake in his family's worries. He was as happy as ever the day Jerry Cassaday stepped into his office and shot him square in the chest. Bruce understood Sharee's desire to buy things, he enjoyed watching her be careless with money for the first time in her life. And most of all, Bruce was proud that she began selling cosmetics door-to-door. An entrepreneur himself, he found Sharee's new profession to be ambitious. Bold. He had no qualms when Sharee brought home expensive dress after expensive dress, and he was nothing but proud when she showed him the computer she claimed was to help her keep track of all her sales.

If you had asked Bruce, he would have said the couple was as happy as could be.

Sharee, evidently, was not happy. Although she was pleased with the security her marriage to Bruce brought, she was bored. She was living the life of a housewife and simply got restless. She started going online and frequenting chat rooms where she could talk to strangers and meet new men. She could talk to these new men and Bruce would be none the wiser.

It was the perfect situation for Sharee. She got to keep the stable home life she knew she needed while engaging in the excitement of meeting new singles and falling in love without the latter threatening the first. In short, she got to have her cake and eat it too.

But this quickly fell apart. Soon, the satisfaction Sharee got from speaking to these men online began to fade. She needed more. She wanted to meet these men, feel their touch. This yearning was fresh in her mind the day she met Jerry Cassaday.

Chapter 5

Jerry Cassaday was working as a pit boss in a Reno casino. Before that, he had been a homicide detective and police officer for the Marshall Police Department and the Cass County Sheriff's Department. He began frequenting online chat rooms after his wife left him. He was lonely and had always wanted a family. He went online hoping to find companionship and an honest connection with a beautiful woman. Instead, he found Sharee Miller.

The two hit it off immediately. For Cassaday, it was love at first sight. He was enraptured by the blue-eyed blonde-haired twenty-something-year-old. There was only one problem: Sharee lived in Flint, Michigan and Cassaday was stuck in Reno, Nevada. They had no way to meet without arousing the suspicions of Sharee's husband Bruce until the perfect opportunity arose—a Mary Kay Cosmetics conference was announced. The location? None other than Reno, Nevada.

Sharee jumped at this opportunity to meet Cassaday in person and the spark they had struck up online burst into flames when they met in person. The two spent every free minute they had together, and Sharee even accompanied Cassaday to work. She would sit at his table and play hands of blackjack. When Cassaday finished for the night, the two would go back to Sharee's hotel room.

While Sharee was honest about being married at the time, she altered many details about her life in Flint to her favor. It was all part of the fantasy she had built up for herself online. Sharee told Cassaday that her husband was a high-ranking member of the mafia who frequently beat her and mistreated her children. They weren't in love, she was just too afraid to leave. Cassaday, who was in his mid 30's at the time, had always wanted a family and was aghast when Sharee told him the details about how her current husband treated herself and her kids. Little did he know it was all a lie.

The picture Sharee painted of her husband Bruce was so far away from the handsome, family-orientated business man that he really was. She wasn't describing reality, she was describing a fantasy. And Cassaday had bought it.

After Sharee inevitably left her new lover behind to return home to Flint, Sharee kept up their flame by sending numerous naked photos by email to Cassaday. They kept in constant touch through emails and instant messages. The two kept in touch so frequently that members of Bruce's family could later recall him complaining about the amount of time Sharee began to spend on her new computer. He knew something was up, he just wasn't sure what.

Sharee continued to build on the fantasy she had created with Cassaday. As well as nude photos, she would send him photos of herself covered in bruise-coloured makeup claiming they were from Bruce. On one special occasion, she went old school and snail-mailed Cassaday a tape labeled For Jerry's Eyes Only...

As Sharee fell deeper into the rabbit hole she had dug, two things became clear to her: the first, Cassaday was completely and utterly under her control, the second, she liked her new fantasy more than her real marriage.

Chapter 6

Sharee Miller's life had taken such a turn from her younger years. She had a stable life, a happy home, and a loving husband. But somehow, this was no longer enough for Sharee. Addicted to the danger of the unknown, Sharee had become bored in her easy marriage. She craved more.

She found the perfect path out of her marriage in Jerry Cassaday. Initially, the thrill of an affair was enough for her, but this eventually grew old—especially when her affair became online only.

Usually, when someone grows tired of their online relationship, they break up with their partner and cease communications. This was not the case with Sharee and Jerry Cassaday. When Sharee grew tired of her online affair with Cassaday she did not stop communications—she increased them. Although she had fallen out of love with the ex-homicide detective, she still needed him for one very specific purpose. He was going to kill her husband for her.

Cassaday had fallen madly in love with Sharee. He believed she was married to an abusive husband who has a high-ranking mafia player. He feared for his beautiful girlfriend and would do almost anything to protect her. Almost wasn't good enough for Sharee though. Sharee was going to use Cassaday to get out of her marriage, and to do so, she was going to have to make him mad first. Mad enough to kill.

Sharee's plan seemed foolproof. Bruce, her husband, was alone at his auto scrapyard a lot, and he always carried a large amount of cash on him, roughly $2000, in order to make change for his customers. Sharee saw this as the perfect opportunity. Someone could easily kill Bruce at his work with no witnesses, and better yet, if they took the cash on him, it would look like a robbery-gone-wrong. This would inevitably point police away from herself. All she needed was someone to pull the trigger.

Chapter 7

At some point during their online relationship, Sharee realized that she had Cassaday wrapped around her finger. She had seduced him in online and in-person and had maintained this enrapturement through sending him endless emails and seductive videos. Sharee began to use this power she had over Cassaday to make him angry. She had already painted her kind, gentle husband to be an abusive mafia man, but she needed more.

About a month after meeting with Cassaday in person, Sharee went to her local pharmacy and purchased a pregnancy test. She knew she wasn't pregnant—she had had her tubes tied after the birth of her third son—but she needed Cassaday to think she was. She went home, took photos of herself with her stomach pushed out, and sent them to Cassaday along with photos of the pregnancy test, which she had drawn lines on so it appeared to be a positive test. To make the lie seem more real, she also sent an image of her third child's sonograms.

I'm pregnant, she wrote Cassaday, with your first children. Twins.

A few weeks later, Sharee sent Cassaday more pictures of her stomach. This time, however, she coated her belly in blue and purple makeup first.

He killed our beautiful babies was the message sent along with the photos.

Cassaday was devastated, his lover's abusive husband had just taken from the world what he thought would be his opportunity to have a normal life with the woman he loved. He fell into a severe state of depression. Cassaday could not take the news. He could no longer watch the woman he loved destroyed by her own oppressive husband. No. He was coming to town to free Sharee and finally have the family he'd always wanted.

Sharee was ecstatic. Through one later-debated series of instant messages, Sharee slowly revealed her perfect plan on how Cassaday should murder Bruce. The whole of Sharee's plan was summed up in only a few damning sentences.

I'll call Bruce at 5pm and tell him to call me when he's leaving. Pull up to the left side of the building, right to the door. He'll be at the desk inside. Take his wallet. Take the whole thing.

Chapter 8

On November 8, 1999, Jerry Cassaday drove from Reno to Flint to kill the man he thought killed his twin babies and repeatedly beat the love of his life.

He followed Sharee's instructions to the word. At 5pm he pulled up to Bruce Miller's auto scrapyard, went inside, shot Bruce in the chest, and took Bruce's wallet. Bruce was on the phone with Sharee at the time, just as she had planned. Sharee had chosen to listen to her husband die.

Cassaday's experience as a homicide detective meant that he could commit the crime without leaving forensic evidence behind. He left the scrapyard office without leaving a single finger or footprint and took Bruce's wallet without ripping the pocket, a general characteristic of a rushed robbery. Investigators were also unable to recover any trace fibers or hairs from the scene or Bruce's body.

After committing the crime he had spent the majority of his life solving, Cassaday turned his car around and headed straight back to Nevada.

Chapter 9

A few hours after listening to her lover shoot her husband, Sharee called her brother-in-law Chuck Miller. She frantically told him that Bruce was missing, he hadn't come home for dinner and his work phone wasn't working. She convinced Chuck to drive out to the scrapyard to check on his brother.

When Chuck arrived, he was affronted with a horrible scene—Bruce was laying face down on the ground dead from a gunshot wound to his chest. His telephone receiver was on the ground next to his face. Within an hour, a full team of homicide investigators were on the scene.

Due to the lack of physical evidence at the scene, investigator's initially had little to go on. The main motive appeared to be robbery, just another day in Flint.

Sharee was brought in for questioning but was never suspected by police. She had been at home all day with her children and several friends. They simply wanted to ask her if she had any idea of who would want her husband dead, and Sharee was prepared for this.

Sharee told detectives that one of her former boyfriends John Hutchinson had owed Bruce several thousands of dollars. Bruce and

Hutchinson had several arguments about this as well as the tumultuous state of Sharee and Hutchinson's former relationship.

Hutchison unluckily had no solid alibi. He quickly emerged as the key suspect in Bruce's murder.

To make things worse for Hutchinson, he had agreed to take a lie-detector test to prove his innocence, but the examination did not go smoothly. In the middle of the test Hutchinson collapsed and ended up going to the hospital. Not only had he failed the few questions he had been asked, but he was so clearly stressed about the test that he had physical symptoms.

The general feeling amongst investigators was that Hutchinson had killed Bruce, they just couldn't prove it. While his autopsy revealed that Bruce had been shot by a 20 gauge shotgun, Hutchinson did not own this type of gun and investigators failed to find one during a search of his home.

Eventually, much to Sharee's delight, the case went cold. It wasn't until a seemingly unrelated suicide miles away took place before police had any reason to suspect Sharee.

Chapter 10

After he returned to his home in Reno, Jerry Cassaday expected his relationship with Sharee Miller to continue as usual. He believed that they would continue to date long-distance until the murder investigation cooled down. Then, Sharee would begin a new life in Reno with Cassaday.

This, however, was not the case.

Sharee barely contacted Cassaday after the death of her husband. She didn't initiate any conversations and stopped replying to his emails altogether. Cassaday, still deep in the world of lies Sharee had created, began to panic.

A few weeks after killing her husband, Cassaday decided to pay Sharee a visit to make sure she was doing okay. When he arrived at her home in Flint, his world fell apart.

Sharee was at home with her three kids and a new boyfriend.

She had double-crossed Cassaday within weeks of the murder. Cassaday instantly returned to the state of depression he had been in when he believed that Bruce had killed his baby twins-to-be.

Sharee and Cassaday never spoke again, and Sharee had almost entirely forgot about her ex-lover when police started knocking on her door again.

Chapter 11

Seven hundred miles away from Sharee and Flint, in Kansas City, Missouri, Jerry Cassaday was found dead in his home, a gun in his hand, Bible in his lap, shot in the head. Cassaday could not live with the crimes he had committed for love, especially knowing that the love he felt wasn't real. It was too much for him.

Before he killed himself, Cassaday took measures to ensure his death would be connected back to Sharee and Bruce Miller's murder. Next to his body, police found his open briefcase which contained his suicide note addressed to his parents and a printed transcript of extensive instant messaging conversations. Outside in the trash, investigators also found a scandalous video of a young woman dancing naked addressed directly to Jerry.

Police showed clips of this video to Jerry's neighbors in order to identify the woman dancing. Several neighbors were able to identify Jerry's online girlfriend Sharee, who lived in Flint. When Kansas City police called the Flint sheriff's office to get more information about Sharee, Flint police were astounded. They instantly knew they had been duped by the blonde, beautiful widow.

When she was identified by Kansas City police, Sharee was immediately connected not only to Cassaday's suicide but also back to her ex-husband Bruce's murder. In his suicide note, Cassaday revealed that he had been the one to kill Bruce. Sadly, it was evident that he still believed many of the lies Sharee had told him. He stated in his note that he had to do it, Bruce had killed his children and that was something he couldn't let go. Even if it meant destroying his own life in the process.

He also described Sharee's role in the murder plot. He stated that she had encouraged him to commit the murder and helped him plan it. He could not have done it without her help. And he had provided investigators with the transcripts to prove it.

Sharee miller was brought in for questioning where she claimed she did not even know Jerry Cassaday. She stuck to this story until police revealed that they had the tape of her dancing, addressed in her handwriting as being For Jerry's Eyes Only. After this, she was forced to change her story. It was undisputable evidence that they had had a relationship.

Sharee then told police she had met Jerry in a computer chatroom while just messing around, trying to figure out something new to do. Computer forensic experts then confiscated both Sharee and Cassaday's computers. What they found inside answered some important questions but raised many others.

Investigators easily found their way into Sharee and Cassaday's private online conversations. They found incriminating evidence on Jerry's computer—the online copy of the instant messaging conversation in which Cassaday and Sharee discussed Bruce's murder. When they confronted Sharee with these messages, she had a planned response: Cassaday was framing her.

Sharee told investigators that in the triangle of herself, her ex-husband Bruce, and Jerry Cassaday, Cassaday was the scorned lover. After she got bored with her online affair, she tried to cut contact with Cassaday, but he wouldn't let her. She claimed that Cassaday had forged the messages to implicate her in something she had never been apart of. Investigators thought that this claim was far-fetched, so they reached out to AOL, the company that hosted the instant messaging service Cassaday and Sharee used to communicate. Surprisingly, AOL took Sharee's side on the issue—it was possible for the messages to have been forged.

Investigators were now tasked with proving the legitimacy of the instant messages that showed Sharee had helped plan Bruce's murder with Cassaday. Under court order, AOL released information about Sharee and Jerry's computer activity. They confirmed that both Jerry and Sharee had been online and logged into the AOL service the same day at the same time for the same length of time as the instant message indicated. Police also found handwritten notes copied in Sharee's writing that listed information found in the messages. If they had been forged, Sharee would not have known this information in order to write it down.

Sharee was now trapped. Although she continued to maintain her innocence, investigators continued to find more and more damning evidence against Sharee.

Sharee had taken steps to cover her online footprints. A day and a half after the death of her husband she had called AOL to change her first name, last name, and her address. After she learned of the suicide of Jerry Cassaday, she did the same thing again. She was clearly worried about the content of her online messages being traced back to her.

Once investigators had confirmed the legitimacy of the messages, they were able to read the diary of Sharee's relationship with Cassaday. They were able to see how she was able to bring Cassaday to a boil, both sexually and emotionally. She brought him into her world the way she wanted him to see it.

Sharee had used her body, in so many ways, to intrigue, seduce, and trap the ex-homicide detective. The only thing that brought her down in the end was Cassaday's conscience on his dying day.

Further, Sharee's actions after her husband's death provided a possible motive for Bruce's murder other than Sharee's freedom. Money.

While Sharee had been loose with money during her marriage, she had gone over-the-top after her husband's death. She used Bruce's life insurance money to dramatically renovate her new inherited home within weeks of his death. She bought herself a new car and spent thousands of dollars on a plethora of items.

When Bruce died, Sharee inherited the family home she had grown so attached to as well as large sums of money both from Bruce's life insurance policy and also from the sale of his auto scrapyard business. Most significantly, though, Sharee had inherited her freedom without having to sacrifice her own and her children's secure, stable life.

Chapter 13

In December, 2000, Sharee went on trial for murder and conspiracy to commit murder.

Throughout the trial, Sharee continued to maintain that the instant messages were forged, as she was innocent of everything. She was simply the victim of an angry lover's broken heart.

The prosecutor's relied heavily on forensic science in their case against Sharee Miller—specifically, on the forensic computer analysis which proved the authenticity of Sharee and Cassaday's messages.

Sharee's trial was a short one. It did not take the prosecutors long to form their case, and the defense presented little-to-no evidence to support Sharee's claims that she was being framed by a dead man.

Sharee was found guilty on the charges of second-degree murder and conspiracy to commit first-degree murder. She was sentenced to life without the possibility of parole.

But this was not the end of Sharee's story.

Chapter 14

In 2009, Sharee Miller was released from prison after serving only nine years of a life without parole sentence. Her release was mandated by a U.S. District Judge who believed that the convicted killer had grounds for a new trial. This was because Jerry Cassaday's suicide note had been presented as damning evidence against Sharee in court despite the fact that Cassaday could not be cross-examined regarding the information in the letter.

Sharee spent a whole three years outside of bars. During this time, she kept a fairly low profile. She stayed in Flint with family, who she spent the most time with. She also spent the three years reconnecting with her sons—the children she spent most of her younger life fighting to support. Sharee's luck finally seemed to be turning in her favor.

But lady luck is fickle. In 2012, Sharee was ordered back to prison by the U.S. Supreme Court. The court disapproved of Sharee's release and mandated that the judge repeals her earlier decision to grant Sharee a new trial. The Supreme Court believed that there was enough additional evidence presented by the prosecutors, with no viable defense to counter it, that the outcome of the trial would have been the same had the suicide note not been presented at all.

Sharee's lawyers told the public that she was simply "disappointed" by her return to prison.

After returning to prison, Sharee and her lawyers quickly filed several appeals targeted at both the decision to return Sharee to court and her original guilty conviction, both of which were lost. Sharee was set to spend the rest of her life in prison for good this time.

That again seemed like the end of Sharee's story until late April 2016.

Seventeen years after manipulating Jerry Cassaday into killing her husband, Sharee Miller admitted her involvement in the crime for the first time through a letter addressed to a County Judge.

In this letter, Sharee claimed that she got caught up in the fantasy world she created with Cassaday. She like being the victim. It was more exciting to her than her real, stable life. However, she quickly found herself in too deep. She had created a monster and the only real way she saw of getting out was through the murder.

If Bruce were to die, neither he nor his family would ever have to discover what she was doing behind his back.

Sharee stated in her confessional letter that she did not enjoy watching her husband die. She wrote, "I had sixteen and a half hours to stop it. And I didn't. I knew it was going to happen and I allowed it. I allowed a man to kill another man based on my lies and manipulation."

She also used her letter as an opportunity to publicly recant the horrible image she had painted of her husband through her messages with Cassaday. She confirmed that Bruce was nothing but a wonderful husband. He had never laid a finger on her, and he always treated herself and her three children with the utmost kindness and respect. She regretted being the reason her children lost such a wonderful father figure—something she had always wanted for them.

While Sharee certainly believed that her confession would put an end to the long-standing controversy surrounding her case, the kind of controversy that inspired both a novel and lifetime movie about her crime, it actually perpetuated a new kind strand of controversy.

To many, especially to Bruce's loved ones, Sharee's confession letter seemed too crafted to be sincere. Sharee was the woman who had manipulated men to kill and die for her all through text. Now, she seemed to be trying to manipulate her way to an earlier release through the same medium.

Whether Sharee will claim another victim as a fool, this time a court judge, is yet to be seen.

KILLERS ON-LINE

76

Mark Chavez

Mark Twitchell

"I was tentative about reaching out because I thought I couldn't offer much and doubted anyone could look past my reputation to the see the human being. But trying is definitely worthwhile if it means finding just one meaningful, mutually fulfilling friendship. My crime doesn't define who I am or represent me at all. I've made some terrible, regrettable choices in the past and I've come to terms with the consequences. Now I seek to infuse purpose into my life. Connection is a huge part of that. My creative engine never slows, so I produce artwork constantly and craft novels or screenplays to manifest my relentless imagination. I'm insightful, passionate and philosophical with a great sense of humor. I enjoy tennis, chess and clever story telling. I love the rain and the music of artists like Sia, Jackie Evancho and Arcade Fire. I'm looking for an interesting, intelligent, open-minded, delightfully imperfect woman to relate to and share amusing observations with...as well as potentially a long weekend every few months if it gets there naturally."[1]

Online dating has become the norm for many of us. Busy lives, children, sometimes working two jobs in order to provide as a single parent, means that it's not so easy anymore to meet people in 'real life'. But this profile is different – this profile belongs to prisoner Mark Twitchell, a convicted murderer who used one of the most popular dating sites around, *PlentyofFish.com*, to lure his victims to an empty garage, where he hoped to satisfy his lust for blood. His first attempt went wrong, and his victim got away – the next was not so lucky.

Mark

Not a lot is known about Mark Twitchell's childhood. He was born on July 4th, 1979, in Edmonton, Canada, to Norman and Mary Twitchell[2]

By all accounts, he had a normal, loving upbringing,[3]but life outside the family home was apparently significantly different and quite difficult for the boy.

Twitchell went to St Cecilia's Junior High, and then Archbishop O'Leary High School, where he was frequently teased and ostracised by his classmates and peers. His nickname was 'Twitch Hell', and the other kids would steal his glasses and taunt him with them, keeping them just out of reach in order to make Twitchell grab for them again and again.

One of his classmates recalled how he would feel unable to help Twitchell as the other kids bullied him.

"I felt really bad for the guy...I remember my dad taught him how to shoot a gun for the first time on a class trip - he could barely hold it after 10 shots. Now people think he's a killer. Unreal."[4]

He graduated from Archbishop O'Leary High School in 1997 and went on to study Radio and Television Arts at Northern Alberta Institute of Technology. He graduated in 2000, and married his first wife, Megan Casterella, on January 4th, 2001. The couple met in an online chat room. The young bride wanted to be close to her sister, so, after they married the young couple moved to Davenport, where Megan enrolled at Palmer College.

At first, Twitchell worked for American TV as a salesman in Davenport, before being transferred to Peoria, some 100 miles away. The couple moved so that Twitchell could be closer to work - however, he still spent much of his time in Davenport.[5]

The marriage lasted four years.

First Divorce

It was not only Megan who took her leave of Twitchell – after working with the company for two years, American TV 'released' him without revealing the reasons why.

The marriage had not been a happy one. When Megan filed for divorce in 2004, Peoria court documents showed that her husband had *"been found guilty of extreme and repeated mental cruelty."* That, plus the spiralling debt of $40,000, spelt the end of the marriage for Megan and Mark.

Although the marriage had been rocky and, by all accounts, abusive, their former landlord, Jody Kimbrell, said the couple had been model tenants – rent was never late, the unit was kept clean and tidy, and there were never any complaints from neighbors. Even after the pair divorced, and Twitchell moved out of the matrimonial home and into another unit in the complex, there was never any cause for concern.

Kimbrell even recalled that there was no friction after the divorce. *"They didn't really speak to each other, but they were cordial."*

Mark Twitchell was an avid Star Wars fan and used to buy and sell merchandise on the internet prior to his divorce.

"Star Wars dolls, paraphernalia, suits, outfits, he had it all – and he bought and sold them constantly...There was Stars Wars stuff all over the unit, but hey, whatever people collect, they collect."[6]

Twitchell's interest in Star Wars wasn't confined to the merchandise, however. Even after he moved to Peoria he remained a member of the 'Quad-Cities Jedi Order', a fan club dedicated to the films. He was also actively involved in Star Wars online forums and groups and was a prolific poster on the boards.

The Dark Side

Although Twitchell's obsessions seemed to be centered around the Sci-fi genre, his wife, Megan, caught glimpses of his more sinister side.

In a book written by investigative journalist Steve Lillebuen, Megan says *"He kind of had that really dark, secretive side...He would make comments like, 'You can't handle what goes on in my mind.'"*

That dark side stayed relatively hidden, apart from the few glimpses Megan caught, for quite some time. Twitchell's time on Star Wars forums had cemented his belief that he should make a fan film about the franchise, and he became more and more immersed in the fantasy, making costumes and spending time at Star Wars conventions.

It was during his marriage to Megan that Twitchell found a new way to have fun. Already well-versed on the internet through both his Star Wars forums and internet dating sites, Mark Twitchell started making up false profiles and tricking people into talking to him – a 'skill' which would eventually lead to something far darker.[7]

However, science fiction had a rival for Twitchell's attention, in the form of 'Dexter' – a TV show about Dexter Morgan, a blood-spatter analyst with Miami Police Department by day, and serial killer by night. Mark Twitchell had found his idol.

Jess

In the fall of 2005, Mark met Jess on the dating website, PlentyofFish.com, and in January 2007, Jess became the second Mrs Twitchell.[8] The honeymoon period came to an end that same year when Twitchell and a former girlfriend made contact on facebook.

Traci Higgins had met Mark Twitchell at the Northern Alberta Institute of Technology where they both studied, in 1997. Their friendship developed, and the pair became a couple. However, Twitchell's dishonesty caused problems in the relationship, and Traci broke it off. But in 2007 they found themselves back in touch – Traci, like Mark, had gone on to marry someone else, and again, like Mark, had gone through a divorce.

The fact that Twitchell had remarried did not deter the former girlfriend, and the pair met up for dinner, with the evening ending with 'a long kiss'. Contact continued between Mark and his mistress throughout 2008, and on October 10th of that year, the pair met up to go to the movies.

The movie, *Quarantine*, was not enough to hold their attention, and instead of watching the screen the couple 'made out' until it was finished, at around 5 pm, after which Traci went home alone. Twitchell, however, had other things on his mind,[9] something Traci would find out about later.

House of Cards

Mark Twitchell still saw himself as a big-time movie producer and harboured dreams of making it big in Hollywood. Towards the end of

September 2008, Twitchell gathered together a film crew, along with a few actors he had found through online casting-call agencies, and they all met at a converted garage he had rented and turned into a filming studio.

Twitchell, now into his third season of Dexter, had written a short film based on the show and called it *House of Cards*. Inspired by the character, Twitchell had turned the garage into his own 'kill room', complete with metal chair, and walls covered in plastic. The story centered on a writer who would lure other men by assuming a false identity on internet dating sites, pretending to be a woman. The killer would arrange to meet the 'dates' at home, where he would jump them, and bind the men with duct tape to the metal chair, which was bolted to the concrete floor. Before murdering the men, he would obtain their banking details and passwords, and once he had their information would brutally kill them and dismember their bodies before stuffing their body parts into plastic bags.

In the eight-minute movie, the killer bought time by using the passwords obtained before the killings to send emails and social media messages to the victims' friends and family, explaining their unexpected absences on a longer stay vacation.

The actor who played the part of the murderer, Robert Barnsley, flew in from Toronto on the promise of a $30,000 cheque for Twitchell's next movie, for his part in *House of Cards*.

The 20-year-old was more than a little surprised by the set-up when he arrived at the garage. The props were real – sharp knives, a stun gun, and a metal table. Although there had been mention of using real blood from a butcher, it was finally decided that they would use corn syrup and red food coloring.

Chris Heward was the actor playing the part of the victim. While he was duct taped to the chair, Barnsley was given a real sword and told to simulate sticking the sword into Heward's chest.

"I twisted the sword to the side, making it look like it was being twisted inside him. I would grind my teeth in the pleasure of killing him."

Heward found the experience unnerving. *"It was very uncomfortable...I was freaking out...I really didn't know these guys. At the time, I was thinking it was really dumb not to bring my agent or anybody with me."*

The final scene of the movie saw the killer sitting at a computer and closing down a fake woman's profile, before putting away a hockey mask – the same kind as had been worn during the murder. When his wife asked him how the story was coming along, the killer replied *"Really well, sweetie...It's true when they say the best way to succeed is to write what you know."*[10]

Lies

Earlier that year, in the Spring of 2008, Twitchell had found himself a job in sales. However, his obsession with his film-making took over and he stopped going to work, without telling Jess. By the time she found out, five months later, the marriage was already deeply in trouble. Their daughter had been born at the beginning of the year, and Jess was sleeping upstairs with the baby while Mark slept downstairs in the basement. He had set up a company called Xpress Entertainment, and was living off the investments backers had put into the company.

When Jess asked her husband what he was working on, in September 2008, he told her it was a film about a man who is having an affair. The premise of the story, he had told her, was that the man had arranged to meet a woman he had met online while telling his wife he was going to the gym. The woman is then attacked and murdered by a masked assailant. When Jess learned that the ending involved the woman being decapitated, she objected and asked her husband to change it.

Jess was quickly learning about her husband's darker side.

The couple, in a bid to solve their marital difficulties, were attending regular counselling sessions together, and Mark was seeing a psychiatrist by himself every Friday evening. On Friday, October 10th, Jess called her husband to ask where he had gone after his session. In a bizarre likeness to the script Jess had objected to, Mark told her he was at the gym. Jess, however, already knew that the gym they both used was closed, and told him so. He then claimed that he was at a different one.

Although the similarities to his story line were striking, there was one major difference. Although Twitchell had, indeed, spent the afternoon with a woman – his mistress Traci Higgins – he had a different kind of rendezvous planned for the evening.[11]

Gilles Tetreault

What nobody realized, however, was that Twitchell had already blurred the lines between fact and fiction. The filming at the end of September had clearly triggered something in his head, giving him the desire to feel what the killer felt.

The filming of the graphic murder scene had gone well, and everyone in the crew was happy with the results – everyone except Twitchell himself. It hadn't gone unnoticed by several members that the director had gone quiet towards the end of the shoot, and only seemed to cheer up when the crew decided that the remaining scenes were superfluous and that they should call it a wrap.[12] Was that when the seeds were finally sown in Twitchell's mind?

It could well have been, because, only a few days later, Twitchell came face to face with his first victim.

36-year-old Gilles Tetreault had been chatting to a woman named Sheena on the dating site, Plentyoffish.com, and she had asked him to meet her for a date. On October 3rd, 2008, Gilles arrived at the garage where Sheena had arranged to meet him. Although he felt it a little odd, he understood her concerns about not wanting to give her address out to a stranger. But when Tetreault entered the garage, there was no sign of the pretty blond woman he had arranged to meet. Instead, he was confronted by a masked man who attacked him with a stun baton, before pulling a gun on him and ordering him to lie down. As the assailant began to duct tape his victim's eyes closed, Tetreault was terrified.

"I started tearing up. A lot of things were going through my head. When they say your life flashes before your eyes, that's what it was. My family. They may never see me again."

Unsure of whether his attacker was going to rob him, rape him, or murder him, Tetreault decided to fight back with everything he had.

"I decided I'd better fight back. I'd rather die my way than his way."

As he began to fight, Gilles grabbed the gun, and, feeling the plastic, realized it wasn't a real firearm. That realization gave him strength, and he took hold of the first thing he could lay his hands on – a pair of handcuffs which had been lying on the floor.

As Tetreault fought for his life, his attacker began to rain punches down on him, but he managed to make it outside. His legs were shaking so much that he was unable to run, though, and he had only made it as far as the pathway when he felt himself being dragged back inside once more.

Tetreault knew that if he was taken back inside the garage again he would be dead, so, gathering all of his strength, the 36-year-old man fought back, again managing to break free from the man who was wearing what he could now see was a hockey mask.

Fortunately for Tetreault, a couple were walking by with their dog and stopped to see what was happening. As Tetreault pleaded with them to help him, the attacker, still wearing his hockey mask, told them everything was ok and that they were just fooling around. The couple left without helping, but it was enough to unnerve the assailant, and he turned and fled, leaving Tetreault to escape.[13]

Once home, Gilles decided to report the attack to the police and logged on to the internet to bring up 'Sheena's' profile as proof. However, the profile had already been deleted and now, Gilles realized, he had no proof of what had taken place, so he made the decision not to, for fear of not being believed.

Gilles Tetreault had had a lucky escape, but it wouldn't be long before he understood exactly how lucky he had been.

Johnny Altinger

Although Mark Twitchell had failed in his quest for murder, the incident with Gilles Tetreault had only strengthened his blood lust. He would try again, and this time he wouldn't fail.

On October 10th, 2008, only a week after his first attempt, Twitchell once again went online in search of his next victim. Plentyoffish.com yielded new prey, and Twitchell struck up a conversation with 38-year-old Johnny Altinger. This time, Twitchell portrayed himself as 'Jen' a 5'6" pretty brunette, who described herself as a hopeless romantic. She invited Johnny to meet up with her that evening, and naturally, he agreed.

Once again, directions to the garage were emailed. In his eagerness to meet Jen, Johnny arrived at the garage 45 minutes early, and, seeing the door open decided to go on in. Mark Twitchell was caught unawares – his kill room wasn't ready and he wasn't prepared when he heard Altinger call out Jen's name. As Johnny ducked under the plastic sheeting, he saw Twitchell, who told him that Jen had said she would be right back. Altinger knew something was terribly wrong, and made to leave, instructing Twitchell to tell Jen that he would come back later.

Twitchell was not going to let a second victim get away. After failing to kill Tetreault, Twitchell had changed his weapon of choice from the stun gun to a lead pipe, and as Altinger turned to leave Twitchell hit him over the back of the head with it, and carried on hitting, bringing it down onto Altinger's head over and over again.

Mark Twitchell had succeeded – Johnny Altinger was dead.

But the murderer wasn't finished. He had set up the garage to mirror the Kill Room in Dexter, complete with a metal table. It was on to this table that Twitchell dragged Johnny's lifeless body.

And it was there that he set about methodically dismembering him, relishing the feeling as he cut, sawed, and hacked his way through skin, muscle and bone, piece by piece.

Mark Twitchell finally had his taste of blood, in every sense. As he stood with his hands drenched in his victim's blood, he calmly ate a candy bar, before continuing with his gruesome task.

Of course, once the body was dismembered it had to be disposed of. Twitchell placed all of the body parts into plastic bags and put them in the trunk of his car. His first plan of action had been to drop them off the bridge into the river, but he changed his mind and instead threw them into a sewer.

His job was still not finished though. In order to deflect suspicion, Twitchell broke into Altinger's apartment and found his laptop. Altinger was still logged in, which made Twitchell's job so much easier, and he sat down in his victim's chair and sent emails to Johnny's friends, telling them he, 'Johnny', had run away to Costa Rica with a girl he had met, and that he would be gone for a couple of months.

He sent a further email to Johnny's workplace, telling his employer that he had resigned with immediate effect.

Twitchell stole the laptop – happy that he had covered his tracks.[14]

The Investigation

Unfortunately for Twitchell, the emails he had sent to Johnny's friends didn't convince them. This behavior was uncharacteristic for the man they knew.

They took the emails to the police, insisting that something had happened to their friend, but at first, the police weren't interested. After all, Johnny Altinger was a 38-year-old man and as such was free to come and go as he pleased. He had no history of mental illness, he wasn't considered a high-risk, and he lived alone, so for a few days, the police did nothing.

His friends would not give up, though, and eventually, the police agreed to investigate. The case made its way from desk to desk, and department to department, until it landed on the desk of Detective Bill Clark, a homicide detective, Clark was unimpressed – in a city with high crime he was a busy man, but nevertheless he decided to take a look, and attended a briefing about the case.

Johnny's friends had continued to receive emails from Johnny.

"I've met an extraordinary woman named Jen who has offered to take me on a nice long tropical vacation...We'll be staying in her winter home in Costa Rica, phone number to follow soon."

However, that phone number never arrived, and the only way Johnny's friends could contact him was via email, facebook, or MSN messenger. When they questioned why they couldn't reach him by phone they were told that the reception was bad.

It was lucky that Johnny had had the foresight to give the directions to the garage to a friend before he set off on his date. The police were able to track down the place and discovered that, rather than a woman named Jen, the house to which the garage belonged was rented by Mexicans, and that the tenant of the garage was a local filmmaker who was using the garage as some sort of studio.

The police interviewed Twitchell – he was cooperative and helpful and seemed genuinely bemused by the case. When the garage was searched, Twitchell was asked when he was last there, and he told officers that he hadn't been there since September. However, one of the officers noticed a lot of cleaning supplies on the table, along with a receipt. The receipt was dated October 15th. Twitchell played it down, claiming that he had forgotten that he had stopped by briefly to drop off some cleaning supplies, which he had forgotten about until then. Something didn't sit quite right. Detective Clark felt that it was too great a coincidence that a man had disappeared on a first date from the exact same place that was being used by a filmmaker. Twitchell was interviewed a second time.[15] The police decided to bring in crime scene investigators and asked Twitchell if he would give permission for them to go over the garage for evidence. He readily agreed, but then offered up some new information. He claimed that, on the night of Altinger's disappearance, he had been approached by a man who asked him to buy his red Mazda for $40. Officers followed Twitchell's directions and found the car about a mile away. The car was registered to Johnny Altinger, and police now had the connection between him and Twitchell.[16]

Apart from the Mazda, Clark found several more flaws in Twitchell's story, but he didn't have enough evidence to hold him, so he was released. Clark had read the scripts the crew had been working on, and had started to see similarities between the story and the disappearance. Although he didn't have enough to keep Twitchell there, Clark did have sufficient cause to seize Twitchell's car.

That was when his story began to unravel.

The Pontiac Grand Am was searched, and police found Twitchell's laptop, along with traces of blood, both in the trunk and on a knife which was next to the laptop. The computer was taken by technicians to see what could be found, and Clark was presented with a 42-page document which had been recovered from the deleted files, entitled 'The SK Confessions'. The first paragraph read: *"This story is based on true events. The names and events were altered slightly to protect the guilty. This is the story of my progression into becoming a serial killer."*

As Clark read on, he discovered that what the police had uncovered was a diary of the murder of Johnny Altinger. It detailed the dating ruse, the murder, and the intention of repeating a murder every Friday night. It also revealed the earlier attempted murder of Gilles Tetreault. However, the one detail Clark wanted more than any other was the whereabouts of Johnny Altinger's body – a detail which Twitchell had failed to record.[17]

Twitchell, still a free man, was put under 24-hour surveillance, with police concerned that he would kill again. On October 20th, 2008, ten days after Altinger's murder, they obtained a search warrant, and as they searched his house Jess took their daughter and left. She found her husband at his parents' house and told him the police suspected him of murder. She also questioned him about an incident which had happened recently, when she had caught Mark looking at a website which offered married people the chance to have affairs. At the time, Mark had told his wife that it was research for a freelance article, but when she confronted him again at his parents' house, Mark confessed. He had even been so devious as to hire an actor to play the part of an editor should Jess decide to check out her husband's story, a fact he admitted that day.

Jess left Mark there and then, and the next time she saw him was when she gave evidence at his trial.[18]

During the search of the couple's St. Albert home, they uncovered several pieces of incriminating evidence. A pair of Mark's recently washed jeans which still had traces of blood on them, and some blank postcards of Costa Rica – the place Johnny Altinger had supposedly gone with 'Jen'.

The search moved on to the garage, which the detectives now decided warranted a much closer look. Unlike Dexter, Twitchell hadn't managed to remove all traces of blood, and not only was there blood in the cracks on the table but they also found a large amount of blood spatter on the door, and less than two weeks later the blood from the garage, as well as the blood found in the trunk of Twitchell's car, was proven to be that of Johnny Altinger.

His Arrest

The police had all the evidence they needed, and on October 31st, 2008, Mark Twitchell was arrested for murder.

When Gilles Tetreault saw the news coverage, he realized that it was the same attacker, and came forward with his story. However, throughout all of their investigations, the police still had no idea where Johnny Altinger's body had been dumped. They brought Twitchell back to the garage in the hope that it would prompt him to reveal the location of his victim's remains, and on June 10th, 2009, he finally revealed where police could find the body by giving them a detailed map leading to the sewer where he had hidden the body parts.

The Trial

On March 16th, 2011, Mark Twitchell's murder trial began. He took the stand as the only witness for the defense, and told a story about how he had set Johnny Altinger up in an elaborate hoax to gain publicity for the movie. When Altinger realized this, according to Twitchell, he became irate and a fight ensued. A fight which led to Altinger's death. It was, Twitchell claimed, self-defense.[19]

A key piece of evidence in Twitchell's trial was the 42-page document, 'The SK Confessions'. He claimed that the initials 'SK' stood for his favorite author Stephen King – when in fact, it was believed that it stood for 'Serial Killer'. The jury heard the document read out loud, listening to graphic details of the killing, and the subsequent dismembering, of Johnny Altinger. There were some details which were held back, as they were thought to be too distressing for the members of the jury to hear. One such passage described how, when Twitchell cut off Altinger's head he played with it as if it was a puppet.

"I grabbed his jaw with my gloved hand and moved it while making a funny voice to make it look like it was talking, and chuckled to myself at the total silliness of it all."

Other details of the document, which Twitchell insisted were fictional, provided further insight into his psyche. He described the moment he cut open his victim's torso and watched the internal organs becoming displaced.

"If I had a sense of smell this might be disgusting for me. But I only find it fascinating...Most people fantasize and it only ever stays a fantasy. They don't have the disposition or the stomach to go all the way with their dark urges. But I do."

Talking of killing in a more general sense, Twitchell went on:

"I do not have any reservations about disposing of the negative people in this world who deserve a one-way ticket to the afterlife if such a thing exists."[20]

On April 12th, 2011, Mark Twitchell was found guilty of murder and sentenced to life in prison with no chance of parole for at least 25 years.

It was decided not to pursue the charge of the attempted murder of Gilles Tetreault, as it would not add to the maximum sentence he had already received.

Twitchell continued to cause controversy from inside Saskatchewan Penitentiary where he is serving his sentence, by buying a flat screen TV for his private cell, on which he was able to continue watching the show 'Dexter' – the same show which had inspired him to murder Altinger and attempt to murder Tetreault.[21]

As Bill Clark put *it "He's reliving his fantasy whenever he's watching that show...It's ridiculous to think that he would be allowed to do that. Maybe he's refining his skills?"*[22]

A worrying thought for everyone, but perhaps none more so than an ex-employer of Twitchell, who was mentioned in the 'SK Confessions', who was described as *"a twisted old fart who hated life and everything in it. I owed it to the world to remove him from its glorious surface and would take my chance when I was ready."*[23]